THE
GOODWILL
JAR

THE GOODWILL JAR

Reflections on
Leadership and Legacy

Nick O. Rowe

Advantage | Books

Published by Advantage Books, Charleston, South Carolina.
An imprint of Advantage Media.

ADVANTAGE is a registered trademark, and the Advantage colophon is a trademark of Advantage Media Group, Inc.

Printed in the United States of America.

10 9 8 7 6 5 4 3 2 1

ISBN: 978-1-64225-856-1 (Paperback)
ISBN: 978-1-64225-855-4 (eBook)

Library of Congress Control Number: 2023917742

Cover design by Matthew Morse.
Layout design by Lance Buckley.

This publication is designed to provide accurate and authoritative information in regard to the subject matter covered. It is sold with the understanding that the publisher is not engaged in rendering legal, accounting, or other professional services. If legal advice or other expert assistance is required, the services of a competent professional person should be sought.

Advantage Books is an imprint of Advantage Media Group. Advantage Media helps busy entrepreneurs, CEOs, and leaders write and publish a book to grow their business and become the authority in their field. Advantage authors comprise an exclusive community of industry professionals, idea-makers, and thought leaders. For more information go to **advantagemedia.com**.

To my loving parents, Farmer and Jane Rowe.

To my lifelong love, my wife, Tyra.
To my lovely daughters, Dominique and Ebony.

I am also dedicating this book to those coming along
in this journey of life, leadership, and happiness.

THE ULTIMATE MEASURE OF A MAN IS NOT
WHERE HE STANDS ON MOMENTS OF COMFORT
AND CONVENIENCE, BUT WHERE HE STANDS IN
TIMES OF CHALLENGE AND CONTROVERSY.

-DR. MARTIN LUTHER KING JR.

CONTENTS

CHAPTER 8

Someone Has to Do It . . . .

CHAPTER 9

Who's Saying Your Name? . . . .

FOREWORD

As iron sharpens iron,
so one person sharpens another.

—Proverbs 27:17

Nick O. Rowe and I met in the lobby of The Hotel Hershey at an American Water Works System Manager's meeting in 1990. I had given a presentation that day, and Nick had sought me out to congratulate me.

I remember thinking how great the conversation was. Nick was authentic, humble, and engaging. He made me feel good about my moment, and I immediately wanted to get to know him better. It turned out we had a lot in common. We were both ambitious, emerging leaders at the time. We were both married to our childhood sweethearts. In addition to just starting our water careers, we were starting our families. And our parents had passed on to each of us a strong faith and the encouragement to lead a purpose-filled life. We both sensed that we needed to get together again. Little did we know that just a few short years later, Nick and I would work together and live next door to each other in what would be a life-changing blessing.

The Bible tells the story of David and Jonathan's friendship. They strengthened and encouraged each other. They celebrated life's joys together. They also mourned each other's losses as their own. They were bound to each other and loved each other as themselves. David and Jonathan lived and loved together as friends.

I know how it must sound—comparing your friendship to a biblical one! I just know that I love Nick with all my being and count his friendship and our brotherhood as a true blessing from God. He has an amazing life story filled with successes as the world would define. But the real success story of Nick O. Rowe is his "servant leadership" and the impact he has had on his family, friends, and colleagues. He is a true force for good, and I am a far better person for it! This book humbly shares Nick's leadership journey, and its truths can change your life as well!

Eric W. Thornburg

July 2023

INTRODUCTION

This book is about doing the right thing for the right reasons at the right time. I firmly believe that everywhere we go, each of us has the opportunity to leave people and places better than they were when we got there. Whether that is at school, at work, at home, or in the community, there are chances everywhere to make the world a happier, more peaceful place.

Some might think money is the definition of success, but even the richest people in the world reach a point where they have all the stuff, have seen all the places, and have done all the things they wanted to do. When that happens, they are left with a choice to turn inward and hoard their knowledge and wisdom or to turn outward and share it. You can have all the money in the world but have nothing in the end. The way you inspire people and make a difference is the real measuring stick of success.

I have always believed the next generation is not only going to be better than the last, but they will also be the solution to many of the social problems we face today. Unfortunately, I have noticed a growing crisis of identity. Too many young people aren't sure of their purpose or where their values lie, but they have so much potential! This book contains the wisdom gathered from decades of being a servant leader and watching as people and environments responded to positivity and true leadership. I think our rising leaders want to do everything they can for the greater good, but they don't know where to start. This is why I wrote this book. I want to be able to say at the end of my life, "I had a good life because I gave back. I'm ready to go."

As I started gathering my thoughts on leadership and interviewing family members, friends, and colleagues, I noticed several themes emerge. The first was the importance of recognizing and building on the foundational value system we gained in our early years. When I look at successful people I know, so much of their decisions go back to good parenting and the principles that are instilled in our youth. For those who did not have the advantage of a strong foundation, I have noticed that successful individuals can point back to another influential individual such as a relative, teacher, or coach who helped shape them. We can't make excuses for making bad decisions if we remember what we were taught as children.

The second theme that I saw was how important it is to put others first. Servant leadership is key. Anyone can be an inspirational leader by having a contagious "you before me" mentality. Every leader can create a ripple effect of positivity all around them while still driving productivity and results.

Having faith in God and a surrender to a plan greater than one's own is another theme that I explored. I am a Christian, so I use the name of God throughout this book, but I hope that readers can attach these leadership lessons to their own belief systems, whatever it may be.

Finally, if you want to build a legacy that endures, you have to think beyond yourself, particularly your family and those who are closest to you. Just like my parents always said, "It's not what we leave to you, it's what we leave in you that really matters."

When I think about servant and inspirational leadership, I think of a wonderful lady I met recently. Jackie Joyner-Kersee is one of the greatest track-and-field athletes in American History—a world-renowned Olympic medalist and deemed the top female athlete of the twentieth century. What I noticed most about her was her humble attitude and her drive to win. What great characteristics for a leader! She is a native of East St. Louis, Illinois, where she founded the Jackie Joyner-Kersee Youth Foundation to encourage underserved youth in her hometown to play sports. She inspires many young men and women to reach for the stars and continue to dream big and have winning attitudes.

Looking to servant and inspirational leaders, such as Jackie Joyner-Kersee, provides opportunities to reflect on our personal journey to better understand how our choices affect others in every relationship we have, whether they be with our family, coworkers, neighbors, classmates, and even strangers.

Now, how can we use those characteristics to make ourselves better leaders? You see people who are winners and good leaders, and they don't have to tell you how great they are. We just know it already. We feel good when we are around them, and we are happy to help them in any way we can. This is, in essence, what the goodwill jar is all about. My hope is that as you read this book, you will learn how to fill the goodwill jar of everyone around you and how to have yours filled in return!

CHAPTER 1

A Firm Foundation

Through our daily walk, we can make things a little bit better in our little part of our little world.

Well, congratulations! It looks like you were successful at getting yourself born. As the newest soul on earth, you quickly learn to manage yourself and the world around you. You crawl, then walk, and then talk, and your parents and other caregivers are always there to teach you and keep you safe. Before you know it, you're in school. This new world of desks and books and other children can be disconcerting at times, but you find that you enjoy it a great deal. You come home every day excited to show your mom the things you did. Your dad asks you at dinner how your day went, and you tell him some of the things you have learned.

One day, the class bully chooses you as his target for reasons you don't understand. He starts calling you a name you haven't heard before, but you know it is mean by the context. When you go home that night, you tell your parents about it. They counsel you on how to handle the situation if it happens again, using many of the words you have heard before from them: integrity, values, kindness, faith, patience, and, above all, love.

The next day, he finds you on the playground and begins calling you that name again. You try behaving in the way your parents told you to behave, but his meanness escalates, and he pushes you down. So much for patience and values, you want revenge. You stand up and hit him back. Before you know it, you are both being hauled into the principal's office to explain yourselves. Parents are called in, and consequences are discussed. As you go through adolescence, you and your parents discuss this bullying incident, and you learn important lessons about relationships, building trust, and self-control. They help you learn how to disarm people with love and kindness so that the next time you are mistreated, you are better prepared. You are guided by teachers who see your potential and other caring adults who act as coaches, counselors, and mentors.

That was not the only difficult experience, by a long stretch, but it was one of the formative moments in your life where you decided you had the ability to control the way people treat you. You can love instead of hate. You can stand up for others who are being mistreated. You can have faith through troubled times. And you can choose the right, even when the wrong seems so appealing.

Building Relationships

I'm a living testimony to the power of empathy.

I lived through the time of segregation and integration in the United States. From kindergarten to second grade, I attended a segregated school in Bowling Green, Kentucky. We lived on the side of town which was predominantly white, and I remember being confused that all the kids in my neighborhood went to the school down the road, while I was being driven all the way across town to go to the Black school. I remember saying, "Dad, the school's right around the corner. Why am I going way over there?"

He'd say, "Yeah, I know. But it's a good school over there that you go to."

I'd say, "Yeah. But, Dad, we gotta get up so early, and we gotta drive all the way over there."

My parents refused to make a big deal of it, so I let it go. I don't remember thinking much more about it until I was in third grade, when the integration happened. Suddenly I was going to the school around the corner with the neighbor kids. Everyone in the class was white but me, including the teacher, so I was the odd man out. People there had not seen anybody like me in the classroom.

There're a lot of hurtful things that happen to kids in the third grade. Children say things or laugh at you. You're left alone at recess, and nobody's playing with you. It happens everywhere, children being insensitive. And it was no different for me. But somehow, even at that early age, I knew I had to find a way to build and maintain trust with the people in my class if I wanted to have any friends.

My breakthrough came when my teacher had a class-wide math contest. She wrote all our names up on one of the two chalkboards, and she would give us a problem. "What is 246 times 24?" That kind of thing. As kids got the problems wrong, their names were erased from the list. I was always really blessed to have a sharp mind, so this was my moment to shine.

At the end of the contest, I was the only name left up on the board. Suddenly the kids in my class started looking at me a little bit differently. I wasn't the odd man out as much now. The math contest continued to the next level, where each classroom winner in the third grade competed against each other to see who would win for the whole grade. Because I was representing my classroom, they were all cheering for me to be the best.

I ended up winning that too. This meant I became the representative for the whole third grade. Boy, did they cheer for me then? By just being myself (which happened to be someone who was good at math), I connected with the rest of the kids. They all wanted to see me win the next round, and the next, and show the whole school that our class had the smartest kid in it. That's how I broke down the walls that were there before. We had common ground. Pretty soon, recess was different.

For some people, building relationships starts a little later, maybe when you're in high school. You start building trust with your peers, your counselors, your teachers, your coaches, or your principal. They become your mentors and confidants. The things you learn from those interactions stay with you into adulthood.

I was the first Black American valedictorian at Bowling Green High School. I have to admit that was a pretty big deal to me. Even now, when I consider all the other awards I have been given over the years, that is still one of the most important honors I was ever given. I went to a big high school, so there was strong competition for that top spot. We were all just an A or B apart to determine who would be number one, number two, and so on. When I was chosen, it was the ultimate validation that my efforts to be a part of this school that I had not even been allowed to attend for the first two years had paid off. I was truly recognized as an important part of my peer group.

It doesn't matter where you are in your journey; we all have to learn how to build those important connections with others. My journey probably isn't that much different from yours. You might not have been the best math student or the valedictorian, but I'll bet you found things that you could use to make connections with your peers and the adults in your life. As we grow from elementary school to middle school to high school, the whole notion of building relationships of trust looks a little bit different at each stage. Then it starts all over again in college and then again in the workplace.

With each shift, relationships bring more complexity and richness into our lives. Children can easily become best friends in the sandbox and never even learn each other's names. For adults to become close friends, there are so many factors that can help or hinder us. Biases, history, similar interests, mood, schedule, personality types, and so on. It's kind of a wonder that anyone can make friends after the age of ten!

But we can, and we do. And we need to continue to build relationships throughout all our lives if we want to live our fullest, richest, happiest life possible. One of the key factors that dictates the way we interact with others (and one that we often forget) is the foundation we were given as children.

Foundational Values

In my home office, I have a photograph of an old Western Union telegram. It reads:

Mr and Mrs Elmo Rowe

Burkesville KY

The secretary of the Army has asked me to express his deep regret that your son PVT Rowe, Farmer J. was seriously wounded in action in Korea on 14 June 52.

WM E Bergin Major General USA The Adjutant General of the Army

My father was twenty years old when his parents received that telegram with no further explanation. They didn't even know if he was still alive or not, or where on the planet he was. They wouldn't learn anything more until he called from a foreign hospital, telling them that he had been hit numerous times and that he was going to be coming home with one Purple Heart and one leg.

To this day, I struggle to hold back my tears when I think of what happened to him as the only Black American soldier returning home on a flight full of wounded soldiers. My friend and Attorney-at-Law Sam Henry knows, so I'll let him tell the story here.

Nick and I were friends since college, and we would visit his family in their home in Bowling Green, Kentucky. We grew so close that I always called his father and mother Daddy Rowe and Momma Rowe. On one of my first visits, Daddy Rowe shared one of the great stories of his life with me.

I remember the day like it was yesterday. Daddy Rowe had all of these medals from serving in the military, and they were hanging up on a wall. I had asked him about each medal, and he was telling me about them. It was like I was getting a history lesson, so to speak, on the medals and his service in the Korean War, and all of those great things. One medal was the Purple Heart, where he had gotten his leg kind of blown off when he was very young.

Then he told me when he was flying back home, everybody on the plane was eating. Somebody said, "Has everybody eaten?" And then somebody else said, "Everybody, but that [bad word] in the back."

Tears ran down Daddy Rowe's face when he told me this. And tears ran down my face. It was hard for me to see the pain that his father experienced after making such a great sacrifice for our country all those years ago. It left a lasting impression on me, and a moment I will never forget.

Every time I think of this, I get pretty emotional. He put his life on the line for our freedoms and came home a war hero, but he still wasn't getting fed on the plane ride home because of his skin color. That hurt more than anything else his whole life.

You know, using that bad word, the N word, has become common today. I've had people ask me, "Why don't you use it?"

Well, that's why I don't use it, and I will never use it. People don't know what words mean sometimes. I know Black Americans who use it. I know white Americans who use it. It's hurtful when I hear rappers use it. Every time I hear it, I think about my father thinking, "I gave everything I had, but I'm still the same guy. I'm still not good enough. Everybody's been fed on the plane except for me."

This was just one of the countless reasons my parents might have been justified to raise me and my six siblings with resentment and even hate for the way we were treated by some people, but they didn't. Instead, I grew up in a home that was full of love and respect. My siblings and I grew up going to church every Sunday with our parents. All I knew was to be a member of a church. Even up to the day my father and mother passed in their eighties, they made church a priority, as much as their health would allow. My testimony of God grew with me, and I can honestly say, it has been one of the most constant forces of good in my life.

My father had numerous wounds from the war and became a carpenter. My mom was a nursing assistant. They lived a good life. We may not have had much by way of material possessions, but we always had enough. My parents were wonderful role models of integrity and love and compassion. They really knew how to treat people right. My parents were married sixty-five years at my mother's passing, so we saw what a loving marriage should be. Because that was my first example of what a husband and wife were, I always assumed I would have the same kind of marriage one day. And I do!

I know my childhood was distinct to me, but I believe everyone is given similarly foundational experiences in their youth that give us the core values that shape the way we live the rest of our lives. Now, I recognize that not everyone is fortunate enough to be born into a home with two wise and loving parents like I was, but I know if you weren't fortunate to be raised in a stable home with devoted parents, it's very possible that you had another adult who taught you values, whether it was another relative, a teacher, a coach, a church leader, a guidance counselor, or someone else.

Most children have many adults in their lives who add value to their lives. For me, one of these adults was my high school principal. He was extremely invested in the future of his students beyond high school. He had a list of jobs in his office, and he would make sure we were all employed every summer. I'll never forget how he would pull out his notepad and say, "Nick Rowe, this is where you're going to work."

Then he would send me off to meet my new boss. Every year it was a different place. I guess if you think about how most high schoolers are, they always want the highest-paying jobs. But he'd say, "No, you're not going there. You did that last summer. You're going to go over here now."

Some of those jobs paid next to nothing. But for him, it was bigger than the money. That first dishwashing job seems just like yesterday. My principal had more perspective than we had. Another one of my earlier jobs was in a factory. I worked at building carburetors on the line on a midnight shift. I had my role to add a certain part and then pass it on to the next person. This job really gave me an appreciation for safety. Even now as an executive, I'm a big safety guy with my employees because I was always worried about getting hurt or having that other person next to me getting hurt. I did that through the school year, where I had to be in an eight o'clock engineering class in the morning, so I learned how to dig deep and keep going, even if I was exhausted.

The factory paid well, and so I wanted to go back to that the next year. The principal said, "Nope, you are going to sell men's clothing now." Like I said, he had the big picture and knew I needed a variety of experiences. He helped me get a position in the department store, Sears & Roebuck. I had to go to work every day in a suit and a tie, which I didn't like. But it taught me what customer service was all about. He taught me to dress for success. Of course, my parents were always great dressers.

I had also been working during my time in high school with my dad's landscaping company, so I knew how to get my hands dirty, to sweat, and to appreciate hard work. It helped me to be able to appreciate people at all levels of any organization, and there isn't any better way than to walk in their shoes. So many things that came out of that journey. I learned that everybody comes from a different place, but it doesn't make you any better because you wear a suit and a tie.

I remember this principal took all of us students to his new house, and I was in awe. I wanted a house like that. I went home and told my parents that one day I would have a house like that. This gave me a dream to work on.

So from having that dream to being able to walk in the shoes of others, my principal added to the foundation that my parents laid for me. He always encouraged me and the other students to follow our dreams. If I had said, "I want to be a rocket scientist," I know he would have encouraged me to do that. It's so easy for adults to shut down the dreams of children, especially when they seem unrealistic. But it's not our job to take those away.

We can be an inspiration to a child and not even know it. The little things we sometimes think are nothing often matter the most. You take somebody younger under your wing and share with them your experience and get them to dream a little bit early on, and before you know it, they are out there fulfilling their dreams.

It doesn't matter where you are in your life journey either. You could be the CEO of your company, but if an employee comes to you and says, "Hey, I want your job," you should say, "Well, I think you could get there, but here're some things you have to do."

If you say, "Oh, you could never do my job," that breaks their spirit. Who are we to do that?

My principal was a dream supporter of the very best kind. Of course, I didn't know what he was doing at the time, but he was helping lay that foundation I needed for the rest of my life. My parents instilled my values, and he shaped my dreams. He inspired and built us all up. These three individuals were instrumental in making me who I am today. They taught me to work hard, respect others, and, above all, love everyone I meet as if they were my brothers and sisters. Love was the common thread through everything I learned.

Disarming Others with Love

I don't know anyone who has been able to get through life without having struggles with others. Whether it's a playground disagreement or an argument with a spouse, we all have times when those relationships get strained. This is where the skill of disarming others can save you.

When I say disarming people, what I mean is being kind and treating them with love no matter what the circumstances are. You find a way to connect with them despite anything that might keep you separated.

You know that certain people have certain views, and so it is important to maintain self-control as you try to build a relationship with someone who probably doesn't have the same values or maybe does not look at things the same way you do. This is especially true in today's society with such distinct political boundaries and the growing animosity we see around party affiliation. It means you disregard the differences and look for what makes you the same. I am a retired African American man. It would be really easy for me to build relationships with other retired African American men, right? Sure. But I know it is equally important to build relationships with people who are different from me. What could I find in common with, say, a young Asian American woman? You'd be surprised.

When you find a way to connect with someone different from you, they take down their "arms," those negative reactions or biases that separate you. This is one of the key factors in building relationships of trust.

If you disarm people when you first meet them, it doesn't matter how different you were to begin with; you automatically start building a relationship, even with people who are really challenging to get along with like a tough neighbor, coworker, or family member. And the first step is to find common ground.

Everyone has a soft spot. You just have to find it. Dig until you reach that common ground. Sometimes it's buried a little deeper than others, but if you are patient, you can find it. Maybe it's health, sports, family, hobbies, or family. Sometimes I lead with, "Remember when our bodies didn't hurt?" I'll start there and build up. Another thing I like to ask people is what they enjoy doing in their spare time. This usually sparks positive feelings that I can relate to. I like golf. Maybe she likes swimming. We can find common ground that we both like to be active in our chosen sport.

Did you know 99.9 percent of every human's DNA is the same? Which means we really aren't that much different. My DNA is almost identical to someone of German heritage. Or Korean. Or Brazilian. At a luncheon recently, I was a guest speaker. I pointed out all the CEOs and said, "John, we could be brothers. Sally, do you know how close we are to being related?"

They all laughed, but it is so true. Everyone sees themselves as different, but we aren't! We have certain characteristics and strengths that are a little different. But in the end, we'll all be the same in heaven anyway. Why not here?

When I was in college, I majored in the field of engineering, which was not a predominantly diverse field for females or people of color. It is more so today, but it certainly wasn't back then. I found myself having to build a lot of relationships and trust. Most of our work was done outside the classroom, studying with my classmates. Nobody wants to study with you if you can't help them, which is to say you don't get included in any study group if you can't add value. I knew that I could figure out the problems and that this would be common ground between me and my classmates, so I started offering to get study groups together.

"Hey, can we get together? I've got John and Sally already coming. Why don't you join us and let's work through these problems together?"

It worked every time. When I did this, I made strong connections with my peer group, some of which I still have to this day.

Shared Experiences

A part of our foundation is what we learn from the world. That's the beauty of this global melting pot: we all begin at the same place and end at the same place, too. But while we're on this earth, we share certain experiences.

One of the factors that experts use to define a new generation is the shared experiences they have. By this, I mean those hugely influential moments that an entire generation has at the same time. For the younger generations, the COVID-19 pandemic will be one of those things. For a generation before them, if they were in

America, it was events like the Challenger explosion and 9/11. I firmly believe that every generation is better than the last despite what anyone says. It's true! The next generation is always a little bit wiser, smarter, and healthier than before. While the shared experiences help define the generations, they also bring everyone together by creating a common history we can all anchor to. Even though my experience of integration was unique to me, my children, future grandchildren and even great-grandchildren will know it as a part of our national history, and they will draw meaning from it as they form their identities and beliefs.

For me, one of the shared experiences that I had with my classmates was the assassination of Dr. Martin Luther King Jr. I was in fifth grade in Ms. Hancock's class. I got home from school one day, and both my parents were crying. Really sobbing, like a family member had died. I didn't really get what was happening. I was like, "Why is everybody so torn up? I know he's a civil rights leader, but gosh, you know, he's not a family member."

My parents sat me and my siblings down and explained what this great man had meant to us as a family and to so many people in America, what he was trying to do for racial equality and for everybody. I understand now that he represented so many of the same values that they had been teaching us.

My parents instill in us the same things he had been preaching. You treat people right. You don't take anything from anybody. You don't make excuses. All you need is an equal opportunity. That's all. You don't ask for anything that you haven't worked for. Accept people where they are, no matter who they are.

Dr. King disarmed people. He was a peaceful example for us all. Sure, you're going to have disagreements along the journey, but the way you react to those disagreements is the key. Do you retaliate?

Do you show hatred? Or do you show love? His message was around love, no matter what. People thought he was crazy. You can't love your enemy! But it tied to the Christian faith that we were raised with. The Bible says to love our enemies, and that's hard.

He embodied all the hope that there would be a better place for everyone if we could all work in peace and work in harmony and love together. I think I get that now, but at the time I couldn't understand.

A few days after the news was the funeral. Ms. Hancock wheeled a boxy television on a clunky stand into our classroom and had it hooked up so we could watch it being broadcast. All the fifth graders were kind of uncomfortable. "Why is she so very emotional over this thing?"

We had talked about it in class as part of the educational process of the fifth grade. I was still the only person of color in the class. Watching that funeral procession gave me a lot of pride because I saw someone who looked like me who was trying to do things right, the way my parents had taught me. I saw how much respect he was given by people who looked different from he did. It touched our hearts to see the tribute that was paid to him. Everyone was so quiet.

I learned that day what matters most is how you finish your life. Who really cares what town you're from or what schools you attended or even what degrees or awards you achieved? We don't need to get excited about our hardships along the journey, as long as we finish strong and do the right things and never deviate from those values.

Dr. King was a huge influence on an entire generation, myself included. We hear it said all the time that we are a product of our environment. I think this is true. If we were hurt, we carry that hurt with us. If we are given joy, we give joy. I like to think of it as a jar—a goodwill jar—that we fill for each other. You'll learn more about where this came from in chapter 3.

Adulthood Does Not Exempt Us

As people move further up in an organization, too often they begin to believe that they are above the values they learned as children. They think, "I'm making plenty of money. I live in a big house. I drive a fancy car. That's why people listen to me and respect me." Truth is, none of that really matters. What matters is how you treat people. And the way you treat people is based on your values.

The thirteen-year-old daughter of a friend once asked her mother, "Would you rather do the right thing for the wrong reason, or the wrong thing for the right reason?"

What a profound question, and one that we rarely stop to ask ourselves. Let me tell you that I know at this point in my life that there is never a right time to do the wrong thing. Always do the right thing. If there is any doubt, stop and think. Chances are you might hear your mom or your grandma is whispering in your ear that she doesn't like what you're doing. What would Dad say about this choice right now? My parents have been gone awhile, but still I think about what they would say about my choices. They're raising me still to this day.

You really never lose the foundation that you are given in your early years. It guides how we impact others in all aspects of our lives. It drives our successes in the workplace. If you want to make the world a little better, even if you're just starting at the beginning, it all comes down to knowing where your values come from, defining them for yourself, and maintaining them in your everyday journey. It means filling the goodwill jar of everyone around you as often as you are able to.

If you do this, my brothers and sisters, you will find that your own goodwill jar is never empty.

Reflection Points

- What values were you taught during your foundational years?

- What do the people from your past whisper in your ear?

- Do I live the values now?

- What would it take for me to compromise my values?

CHAPTER 2

Who Do You Think You Are?

You're not as special as you think you are.
You are much more!

You have finally made it to your twenties and have the chance to build on that firm foundation you were given. You look back on everything so far, and you realize that you had a fabulous childhood. You spent the first few years learning how to operate your body—to walk and talk and feed yourself. The next several years were all about learning how the world around you worked through interactions with your environment, your family, your peers, and your teachers. Sure, there were decisions to make, but the stakes were pretty low. If you ever really messed up, there was always someone there to help you recover. Life was good.

But now you're in your twenties, and you realize that you're confused. That foundation doesn't seem so simple when you have little clear direction and even less certainty. And everyone says these are supposed to be the best years of your life. You look in the mirror sometimes and wonder why it's so unfair. No money. No answers. No time. Everyone expects you to decide who you want to be and what you want to do. And remember not to take your youth for granted, they say! But then they ask if you have met anyone yet. Didn't so and so already get married? And how's school? Where did you say you go to again? Oh, that reminds me, did you see that one girl from high school already graduated from medical school and has a six-figure job? Don't worry, they say. It's OK to not have everything figured out, but have you started building your 401(k)?

You are not a quitter, so you remember your roots and dig a little deeper, just like your parents and your grandparents taught you. But at work, you feel like you have to please everyone else, and your voice is muted. Before long, it feels like your identity has fallen into a black hole. Who even are you anymore?

This Is Normal

It isn't uncommon for young professionals to feel like they are losing track of who they are, what they want to be, and where they thought they were going. We know all our decisions impact others. This is why I want to talk about identity. Not many young people enter the workplace knowing who they are, what they stand for, and what they want to achieve. But it doesn't have to be that way!

If you want to rise to become a leader, this stage is the best time to start walking the path of discovery. As you figure out what makes you tick—so to speak—you will develop a vision that is uniquely yours. Your motivations become clear to you and everyone around you. This is what people mean when they say "personal brand."

That term is getting a little worn around the edges, I know. We've been hearing about it since 1997 when the term appeared in Fast Company magazine. Management guru Tom Peters published an article titled "The Brand Called YOU" where he suggested that we are all marketing ourselves every moment of our lives, no matter what industry we work in or where we live. This rocked everyone's world.

I believe that the idea of a personal brand is just as important today as it was back then. Probably more important. With so many choices available at lightning speed, and knowledge expanding by the millisecond, it's so easy for young people in this phase of life to get lost in the flood of options. The pressure is so great, and there seems to be a prevailing message that if you don't do everything right the first time, you're going to get stuck behind and fail for the rest of your life.

This is ridiculous, of course. I can't help but to think about my daughters, who are beginning to move from the early stages of their careers, so I asked them if they have any advice to their peers who are just starting out. My youngest, Ebony, said something that I thought was very wise.

> You don't have to know everything right now. Nothing is permanent. I might try this role for a year or two, get something out of it, and decide I've gotten enough from that. Then let's try something else. I think as long as you keep that mentality, then you don't really have that pressure to feel like you have to have it all figured out. You don't necessarily need know your 20-year plan right now. I just don't think it's realistic. You're always growing and changing who you are. So your interests are going to change as well. It's OK to feel that way.

Her sister, Dominique, added:

Sometimes people worry so much about making mistakes at this point in life. But as my dad always says, "It's just another arrow in your quiver." Or, if you prefer, another tool in your toolbox. Even if you don't like it, you're going to learn something from it, and that makes the lesson valuable. It's something else you put on your resume. You'll learn a skillset that will help you at some point in your life. Even if it's not what you want to do, it can still teach you something. It's a growth point. Use it for your advantage, and then figure out the next step. Or, if you don't know, open your mouth, and ask the people around you that may know. It's OK to say, "I don't know what to do. Help me."

I wish someone had said these things to me when I began my career!

You Don't Get to Choose

Here's the thing about your brand, you're not really in charge. The world is. You can create the brand you want and define what it stands for. However, the way your brand is perceived will depend upon whether you live up to that brand's promise. It's your actions that set your brand. It is what the rest of the world sees in you that matters most.

I'm at the end of my career now, so I don't get to say, "I was really good at my job, guys." That reputation was set up a long time ago based on my actions, my words, and the way I lived my values. I learned in my career that it is the opinion of others that really determined what I was worth. Was I a person of integrity? Did I put something in the goodwill jar of other people? You get to decide.

When I was close to retirement, I didn't have the right to say in the last two months, "I'm going to really enhance my brand." No way.

Too late. At that point, my brand was already built. It was already set in stone.

So often the advice that we see in the world is about building your online presence and your social media platform, all that other stuff. There will always be a distinction between the way the world perceives you and the way you think the world perceives you. Hopefully, if you're very self-aware, that gap is pretty narrow. Unfortunately, for many young professionals, it's pretty wide because of the disconnect in understanding how to truly build a brand. The world will tell you that success can be measured by likes, retweets, and thumbs-up. Don't get me wrong. If you enjoy social media and find that it is opening doors of opportunity for you, by all means keep it in your life. But remember what really matters in terms of evidence of who you really are is the way you've touched hearts. A strong recommendation from another person who knows you well will always be more respected than a list of achievements. There's no evidence of that other than how people feel.

In truth, none of that is your brand. Your brand is what you leave behind with the people that you just interacted with. It's what people remember about you when you walk out of the room. I like to tie it to your character and how you've treated people.

If you've watched many movies, you'll often notice a theme played that accompanies a person or object. These are called "leitmotifs" and are used to communicate emotions about the character or thing. Think about it like a theme song for a person. For example, in Star Wars, we can compare Luke's theme with Darth Vader's. One represents the good side, and the other is evil. If we think of our brand as a leitmotif, this means we don't get to decide what it sounds like.

As a father, there is no higher praise than to hear how the world perceives my daughters. I can see how my daughters are building their brand based on how they're treating people, and I hear the things that others say about them. Sure, they are highly successful engineers, but it seems like nobody ever talks about that. Instead, they say things like, "Boy, she's always helpful," or "She is always giving of her time to others," or "I always feel good when I'm with her."

Your brand (and the source of your own self-esteem) is built around "them" and not "you." If you remember that in every interaction you have, you almost won't be able to help but to build a reputation of integrity, compassion, generosity, and empathy.

It Takes Work

Building a brand doesn't just happen. No. It takes work. Hard work.

I wish I could just let everybody in America know that we're all building our brand every single day, so we need to put more effort into it. Whether you're with a neighbor or a coworker or a friend, it doesn't matter where you are, where you sit, or what your title is. It takes work to build a positive brand.

When I was CEO, I used to talk to our employees about their brand and the way it could help them in their future. I'd say, "Hey, are you going to be where I'm at one day? Then build your brand today."

Do you do what you say you're going to do? Can people depend on you? Do you have enough personal integrity not to steal your company's time by doing your own things when you should be working? What kind of effort are you putting into this?

I used to tell my daughters all the time that you play the game till you make the rules. Of course, you have to always be ethical in everything you do. Don't do anything that's immoral, but you have to learn to play the corporate America game—whatever that means in your industry. You might not like it, but the fact of the matter is you can't change the system until you get in the system. Whether it's the metaphorical shaking hands and kissing babies or if it's networking with the right people or if it's attending a meeting or event that you don't think will benefit you.

There's a time and place to buck the system. My daughters are both Black female engineers, so they are definitely in the minority. They have both worked their way up to a point where they are starting to be able to change that system from the inside out. Once you have the seat at whatever table you need, then you can start to make changes in the way that you want to.

I know this sounds harsh, but at the beginning of your career, you're probably not in a position to be able to throw out the rules yet. You have no leverage, and nobody's going to listen to you. That's just life. But once you get to a certain point, you can do that. Hang in there and be smart. When you have built your brand in a way where you have a rapport with the right people, you can get their ears, and you will be heard. But you have to have that relationship of trust with them first.

Your Presence Is Your Brand

Relationships of trust are built on actions. When I started my career, I was in the railroad industry. I was assigned to be a surveyor in the coal field country, which is a super tough area to navigate. These are places that have the word "holler" in their name, and they have only one road in and one road out. People in these isolated places want to deal with the "known." Everyone coming in from anywhere else is an outsider, no matter what.

I knew I would have to return to these places many times, so it was very important to get them to accept me, even though I wasn't from this area. This is where my presence was critical. I couldn't go in and just expect their respect. They didn't care who I was or what I was trying to do because they didn't know me. Truth was, they would pretty much have been happy if I had left them alone. But I couldn't. We had essential tasks we had to complete on the railroads, and the people living near those tracks and stations were the key to our success.

I learned pretty quick that I couldn't go in there with a chip on my shoulder. I couldn't think I was better than them either. Because I didn't look like them, talk like them, or act like them, I couldn't press them for anything, or they would shut down. I had to find common ground and approach them with humility and gentle understanding.

To address this, I started just sitting in their diners and giving them my business. I would listen to the local talk and expect nothing in return for my money more than a meal. Of course, they were a little curious about me. Suspicious too, but that was fine. They knew who I was because of the company truck, so I didn't have to make a big deal of it. Everyone would size me up, and I had to be OK with that.

My job was to sure not to give them any reason to worry. I smiled at them and asked them about their lives. What was their family like? What sporting events did they enjoy? We tend to think of relationships in terms of 50/50—you give half and I'll give half. With these populations, it was more like I give seventy and they might go the other thirty if I'm lucky. I learned to be gentle in my approach, and when I was, they started to open up. I had to be very, very grateful for even the smallest things. This experience enhanced my character a lot because, boy, they'll put you right in your place if you step even a little out of line.

I call this building your brand of delivery. I tried to be a calm presence. People out there learned that they could trust that if I said I was going to do something, I would do exactly what I said. They also learned that I wouldn't be that person who would complain or bother them when things didn't go perfectly. Which was a lot. It wasn't easy, but I could hear my dad whispering in my ear, "Stay humble, son."

Your brand of delivery is a crucial part of the reputation you leave with others. We've all known those people who have that certain "it" quality that is hard to describe. When they walk in a room, immediately everyone knows they're there and they don't even have to say a word. That presence that they have is unmistakable. These are the people who have perfected their brand of delivery.

We've probably all known those people who do the opposite as well. These are the folks who walk into a room and suck all the life out of it. They drain everyone around them. You don't need to worry about your ability to discern the difference.

Look for those shining stars in your day-to-day life because they are everywhere. You'll know it when you see it. Sometimes it's the person behind the fast-food counter or the one checking you out at the grocery store.

I talk to a lot of high school and college athletes, and some are going to go pro and make millions of dollars. I tell them that they are building their brand every day, but their brand is not built on just how good they are as an athlete. It's really built on how they're treating people. How much do they volunteer? How much do they help their community? Were you the person who was always helpful to other students? Did you cause any problems for the principal or for your teachers? Were you the ones whom teachers always called on?

The beauty is that once you understand how to use your presence to its fullest capacity, you really never lose it. You don't have to be in the forefront of a crowd or on a stage. No matter where you are, people will be attracted to you for reasons that are beyond explanation. The best way to sum it up is that they are drawn to you because they feel good when they're with you.

You're Not That Important

Too many managers and executives think their title automatically makes them a leader, but in reality, nobody cares about titles. They don't matter. Org charts lie. People only care about how you treat them and how inspiring you are. People naturally acknowledge true leadership. You can't demand it. It is earned.

Recognition comes to true leaders because they have the presence of a leader, regardless of their title. Think of it this way; if there's a fire in a huge office building, who is the one person whom all the other people will follow? Is it the CEO who claims he knows what to do, or is it the associate who has proven time and again that she is intimately familiar with the people, with the organization, and even the building? If she says, "There's an exit this way," everyone knows they can trust her. Who will you follow: the person standing in the doorway screaming about his title or the person who is calmly walking toward the exit?

When you think of it this way, you realize the role of a personal brand in leadership. When I was working for the utility industry, I remember one man who was promoted to the position of COO. There was a big announcement sent out that he was coming to visit the area, and when he arrived, he expected to be treated like a VIP. I took him around and introduced him to everyone, but it became clear pretty quickly that nobody knew who he was or nobody cared much about his visit. They politely said, "Nice to meet you," and walked off.

In some cases, they asked him if he was working for me, which was a little embarrassing. But they knew me because I was there with them every day and knew their lives. They knew I cared about them. He left a little humbled because, even though everyone had read the announcement, they didn't care. It was just words. The happy ending to this story is that he learned from that experience and has grown into an amazing servant leader who is making many positive changes in the world. I'm very proud to know him.

I found this happen time and again out there in the coal country. These multimillionaires would fly in on their helicopters to discuss the railroad design or whatever, and here I am, just a young man with a clipboard. And yet I was the one whom everyone came to talk to because they know I could navigate the relationships.

When you're young, it's easy to get caught up in the thought that you have to be better, faster, richer, and more talented. But you'll never win at that. There will always be someone who is better than you at everything. If you're "better," there is always a "best" somewhere else.

What nobody can beat you at is being you. When you build your brand in the right way, people will want to be around you. They'll want to go to dinner with you. They'll want to play golf with you. They'll want to study with you because you're that person.

I want to acknowledge the instability of this phase of life for a moment. Change is inevitable. No matter when you start your career or where you work. Things aren't like my day, when people would stay with an organization for thirty, thirty-five years. Unless you are in the extreme minority, that's not going to happen. I have observed that people change jobs every four or five years now. And every time you change jobs, you get out of your comfort zone again. How you navigate the uncomfortable zone is a part of how you build your brand.

I have met people who are just oblivious to this. They could have the highest status, but nobody wants to be with them. Nobody wants to go to dinner with them. Everyone screens their calls and texts. They think, "I'm sure anyone would be honored to have me." But no, we really wouldn't be. These people are too busy patting themselves on the back and thinking about how much they have to notice that they are all alone. Nobody cares about status. They really don't.

I mean, think about it. Let's say you were the CEO of whatever company and you drove around town with a bullhorn telling everybody in town what your title was. "I'm the CEO of the Generic Corporation XYZ. Look at me!"

People on the street wouldn't care. They'd say, "Why is he doing that? I'm on my way to get dinner, and that's all I am worried about right now. I wish he'd shut up."

I tell my fellow retired executives this all the time, and it really gets their attention. But then they sit back and think, "I guess they really don't."

Everybody's just trying to take care of themselves and their families and do the best they can. We're all about the same, no matter where our hierarchal status is. I really admire the people who pick up our trash because when our trash is delayed for a week or so, people go crazy. They're so important now, aren't they? I think if we just make sure we treat that trash collector as good as we do the next person, that's the key. In comparison, what would happen if you don't go into work tomorrow? They're probably going to be OK, depending on what you do. Now is the time for you to be very aware of what you mean to others and how much potential you may be leaving behind.

Be Humble

We might not be as good as we think we are. But at the same time, we're often much, much better than we give ourselves credit for. I think we often forget how amazing we really are. We never quit this journey of learning and understanding. The more mature we become, the more we realize what really matters and what doesn't.

The key is being humble about it. I like to think that humility doesn't mean thinking less of ourselves. It just means thinking less about ourselves.

I met a gentleman at an event who had a long history of doing things nationally with Dr. Martin Luther King and other amazing people. But he never told me that when I was talking to him. Somebody else had to tell me.

When I saw him again, I was like, "Why didn't you say anything?!"

He said, "Well, it wasn't really that important."

I was stunned. If I had worked with Dr. King, I think I'd want to shout it from the rooftops. But true leaders know who they are and can relax into that knowledge without having to boast. I heard an interview with Tiger Woods' son that shows this kind of confidence. This young man was asked about his dad's performance that day, and he responded, "He's getting better." I was charmed that Tiger's son was totally oblivious to who his father really was. We're talking about one of the best golfers in history here, but he didn't need to boast about it, even to his own family.

I'm even learning this from my own family. I have to brag on my daughter Ebony for a moment. She is a multiple record-holding basketball player with more awards and trophies than we had shelf space to display them. But for all her accolades and achievements, she used to say, "I'm really not as good as people say I am dad." She didn't listen to the noise. All that she focused on was her performance and her potential to improve.

There is so much potential in each one of us! I remember when I met my good friend and Chief Global Officer Valoria Armstrong. She made an impression on me immediately as being a bright, capable, and driven young woman, so I invited her to have lunch one day to offer her a job in my organization. I asked her if she remembered that meeting and what happened, and she was happy to share a few thoughts. She said:

Mine was not your typical career path. Having sponsors, people that are talking for you when you're not in the room, made all the difference for me. I didn't have the extensive operations background that probably others would've had, but Nick took a chance on me in this position. He didn't need to either. When I first met him, we were at a lunch and he must have seen something in me at the time because he said, "I'm going to keep an eye on you. I have a really good eye for talent."

And literally I told him, "I'll never come work at your company."

What's funny is that I became the president of that company! I was not looking at it from the lens of the possibilities. That one comment could have turned him completely off, but he was able to look past all that cockiness. Sometimes we think that we are a little bit more than what we truly are.

It took a little convincing for her to come and join us, but I am so glad she did. She had the humility to swallow those words and see how her career would benefit. Humility is about understanding that none of us are really as good as we think we are, but we're sure not as bad as we think either. Unless you're a narcissist who thinks they're good at everything, we can be pretty hard on ourselves. Our greatest weakness is when we're embarrassed or think we are bad, often we're not. But then the things that we think we're really good at, maybe we're not as either.

Advocate for Yourself

In my talks with those highly talented athletes I mentioned, I always remind them that it doesn't matter where you are working, from corporate America to a bookstore to driving a garbage truck for a living. Your brand is your brand, and your values are your values. Have a vision for what you want to become and hang onto it.

I always believed I was going to be the president of some company despite what everyone around me said. I would talk to

African American leaders at the time, and they would say things like, "You probably aren't going to be the president. It's OK. You don't have to make it that far."

Their message was that I shouldn't dream too big, but I didn't listen. It is important not to back down on what you know you can achieve just because nobody else believes in you. No matter what hurdles you face, keep your faith.

I know it can be really hard at this stage of life. When Dominique started graduate school, she has pretty confident in her abilities. She graduated with her bachelor's with honors, so a master's wasn't too scary. She got humbled from day one. She said:

> I remember sitting down in one of my engineering classes on the first day and it was one of those cases where the professor said, "Look at the person on your left. Look at the person on your left. One of you are not going to be here by the end of the semester."
>
> And I was like, "OK, dude, whatever."
>
> I took the first test I bombed. I've never failed a test so bad in my life. I remember calling my dad, crying, and saying, "I don't think I have a degree. I know I graduated, but I don't think I learned anything. I just bombed the first test." I was really second guessing myself.
>
> And he said, "Are you done?"
>
> "What do you mean?" I sniffed.
>
> "Are you done crying?" he asked me.
>
> "Yeah, I guess."

Then he said, "OK, good. Go to the office and talk to the teacher. Call me back when you've done that."

And he hung up.

So I went and talked to the professor, who told me he always gave a really hard test to start. He said, "Everybody bombs it because I want to see who's willing to stay and work through it."

I said, "But I had a 42%!"

Inside, I was thinking, you shouldn't see a 4 in front of your grade. Jeez, just put F.

But he said, "I know. That's part of it. You're going to have to work your way back and figure it out."

So I had to dig really deep, and work harder than I had ever worked because I was committed to getting that A in the end. And I did!

When you know your personal brand, meaning what you are really made of, what you are capable of doing, and where you are heading in life, you can advocate for yourself when you encounter challenges. It makes speaking up on behalf of yourself the same as speaking up on behalf of others.

Living Your Brand Brings Peace

Imagine a mansion standing next to the most rundown shack you have ever seen. In front of both is a grave that looks the exact same. That's really how simple it is. We all end up in the ground, so what do you want to be saying about your life in the end? I think the goal is to be able to say, "I had a good life. I made a difference. I gave back some of the blessings that I was given. OK, I'm ready to go."

But just think about it. You can have all the money in the world and yet have absolutely nothing of true value.

For a good part of my career, I had to travel a lot. In my local airport, there was a shoeshine, and one day I had a few extra minutes, so I decided to sit down at his stand. On this day, I was stressed because I was going to a business meeting at the corporate office where I would have to present on something I didn't know as well as I wished, and I was not exactly confident.

As I got my shoes shined, the man looks at me and said, "I feel sorry for all these guys. Look at them. Everybody's rushing around."

Of course, I was one of them and I'm thinking, "Wait a minute. I have a nice suit on here. You're shining my shoes. And you feel sorry for me?" So I said, "Well, sir, what do you mean?"

He says, "You guys are running like crazy, but the one thing you have all forgotten about is that you don't have peace of mind."

I was speechless. This man had given wisdom that I couldn't get anywhere else. Ever since, I always tell people to stop and see the shoeshine guy. He'll speak from the heart and teach you lessons you really need. He's going to give you a little faith for the day. To this day, I still see him from time to time and make sure to stop and shake his hand. Note to self and all: "Always stop to see the shoeshine guy."

God sends us messages every single day if we would just listen. These messages can become parts of our identity. My wife, Tyra, is an amazing woman and often reminds me of the lessons I learned as a young man. She and I met when she was only sixteen, so in a way, we really grew up together. She knows that we work on our brand as a family and individually. We used to tell our girls, "Your last name is Rowe, and people are going to always remember you as a Rowe. What you do reflects on all of the Rowe family. Think about your parents and your grandparents. What they lived by, how they lived their life, and how they raised their kids. Always treated people well."

When they would walk out the door, my wife would always remind them, "Remember who you are. Stay true to yourself." I can't think of a better way to put it.

Reflection Points

- If you were to write your own obituary today, what would you want it to say?

- Where do you stand for? What do you stand against?

- If you pay attention, God is sending you signals all day long. What is He trying to teach you right now?

CHAPTER 3

The Goodwill Jar

It's all about investing in relationships.

You throw that weird graduation hat in the air for what you think might be the last time. As it lands, everyone is crying. You've finally made it. You can walk out into the world with your hard-earned degree in hand, ready to tackle anything, and build that brand you know you are capable of building.

This moment is so surreal, but you can help wondering, "What now?" All those voices you had in college telling what you're supposed to do and where you're supposed to go are no longer there. Looks like you're going to have to figure out the rest on your own.

You can do this. You get your first "real" job and are working your way up in your chosen field, slowly but consistently. You know that it's important to work hard and long at this point to make sure everyone knows your brand. But there is so much noise about what is "right" and "good." Remember to exercise and meditate. Make time to socialize with your friends. Keep in touch with your family. But don't depend on them too much. Now is the time to date, but who? It seems like with every passing day, you have more and more expectations to "settle down." Yes, you are expected to settle down, but at the same time you are also expected to work harder and do more. There's no way to win.

You are in the middle of learning how to build relationships with those close to you, such as your coworkers, your boss, and your clients. Some of their personalities really rub you wrong. Sure, you hope to build a reputation for yourself that reflects your values, but mostly, you are just taking things one day at a time and hoping not to get too many people mad at you. What more can you do?

The Goodwill Jar

When our children were in elementary school and started learning to read, my wife put out a little glass jar in the kitchen. She and I put little notes of love and encouragement for the girls sometimes. Then they started doing the same. "I love you, Daddy," or "Mom is the best."

The four of us were always close, but this little jar made a difference in the way we treated one another. It strengthened our relationship and offered evidence of our love for each other. I know now that our relationship with our grown daughters is unusual in comparison with a lot of people. When they were growing up, the four of us did everything together. Today, we still do.

That glass jar was physical proof of our wonderful relationship. This served as a reminder to be thankful for one another. When one of us had a bad day, we could look at that jar and remember that someone cared for us. When we had an argument, that jar was evidence that, at one point, we must have gotten along.

Everyone has an emotional bank account where you store the good and bad feelings that you get from other people. I like to refer to this as the "goodwill jar." I started using this phrase as a supervisor at work. I always really liked the idea of adding things to the goodwill jars of the people in my life. When I wash the dishes after dinner, plunk! I drop a few metaphorical marbles (or pennies or beans or whatever!) into my wife's goodwill jar. I take on an extra assignment for a coworker so they can go home early, and plunk! I've added some to theirs. You get the idea.

But then there are times when you have to take some things out of their jars. I need to give my coworker some tough but honest feedback and whoosh! There goes some of the goodwill. Or I get into a disagreement with my wife about where to eat. Whoosh! She now has less goodwill for me than she did before.

I try to put a lot in the goodwill jar of others. This practice emerged from my belief in doing a little bit of good every day. Being a little bit better than yesterday. Improving all the time.

It doesn't matter what level you're at; whether you're a CEO or a founder or someone working on an assembly line, you can build people up. It has nothing to do with titles. It has everything to do with being a good person. And it never stops. That's the thing about a goodwill jar. It's not like you can say, "OK, I'm done now." No. You have to keep filling those jars up.

It's so easy, too. Just saying something nice can improve anyone's day. I mean, think about how many times someone was nice to you, and you said, "Boy, I needed that today. I don't know who that person was, but today was the day I needed that." You know? I think we all have those opportunities. This comes from the foundation of how we were raised.

In a way, everyone has a metaphorical goodwill jar in their hearts. The thing about your goodwill jar is that it holds infinite compartments, one for every person you come across. It holds the proof of the relationships you have, and it stays with you for your whole life.

In every interaction, every day, you are either adding to or taking away from the goodwill jars of others. When you do and say nice things, your goodwill jar increases, which is useful when you know you are going to have to do something that will deplete it. Maybe you have to disagree with someone or give difficult feedback. This takes away from the goodwill. If you have built the goodwill jar up ahead of time, that challenge won't break your relationship because there will still be goodwill left.

The cool thing is that when you fill the jar for others, you are automatically filling your own. You can't help but to love the people you serve.

Let's use and example. Your goodwill jar with your mother, let's say, is enormous. It holds everything she did or didn't do for you from the moment you were born. And hers is the same for you. Everything you have said to her, given her, asked of her, and inflicted upon her is there in her goodwill jar.

Constructive feedback sometimes hurts. When you have a full jar, it's going to be OK. You do the right thing; then when there is an issue, the dialogue is already positive, people will offer their compassion much quicker. A full goodwill jar brings benefit of the doubt rather than skepticism or resistance. When you've been married forty years like me, you've learned to put some in every day. If we screw up, and we always do, our spouse will dump stuff out of our goodwill jar real quick!

And that's the thing about the goodwill jar that you need to know. It is always changing. A full goodwill jar has a whole lot of love and positivity in it, so when you need to go to that person and ask them to take some out by doing you a favor or meeting a need that you have, there is plenty to spare. It operates kind of like a bank account. You can't make a withdrawal if there's nothing there.

My friend and colleague, COO Bruce Hauk, said:

> As a leader, you have to be intentional because it can sometimes be lonely at the top. It is easy to get down or overwhelmed with all the challenges and pressures to deliver, but you have to be that person of positivity and inspiration. This is where the goodwill jar is very important regarding personal and professional relationships. There will always be withdrawals that need to take place from time to time with the people you lead and work with. In those relationships, you need to be at a point where you have built enough trust first before making a withdrawal. You need to have invested in those individuals before you can expect them to trust you and realize that you have positive intent in your counsel.

Doing this makes it possible to have a disagreement without being disagreeable. You need to ask your boss to move an important meeting to accommodate your schedule? If your jar is running low, they might not be so pleased to help with that. You need to ask your neighbor to take better care of their dog, and you know they won't like your request. Again, if you've never worked to fill up their jar, there's a chance they will say no. And they probably will say a lot worse!

This also applies to people whom we don't know very well. In fact, I would suggest it matters more than you can ever know. A smile can brighten an overworked server's day. A friendly greeting might be the only kind words an elderly person hears all day. A kind word to an intern even has the potential to change their entire career.

If you have made sure to keep those important goodwill jars full, life can be so good. You'll find that people are happy to help you when you ask. Even more, they will often want to go above and beyond to please you because they care about you. Keep those jars full to overflowing!

But how?

No Scorekeeping

I know I just told you that the goodwill jar is like a bank account, so you might be tempted to think about it in numbers. This isn't the case though. It's not about give and take. It's about give and give.

When there are things to be done, two people with full jars will share in the responsibility. Both sides have to do their part and take ownership of the relationship. The best relationships are those where nobody keeps track of who did what last. There is no scorecard keeping record of favors and requests.

None of that matters. The first thing you can do if you want to fill someone's goodwill jar is ignore who did what and when. So what if you have done the dishes the last three times. Goodwill is about loving and giving with no strings attached. If you go ahead and do those dishes a fourth time without complaining, and then maybe a fifth and a sixth, you are adding a drop to the goodwill jar of anyone you live with.

Now, I know what you're thinking. "But at some point, somebody else has to do those darn dishes!" Yes, I agree. By letting you do them all the time, they are certainly taking a lot out of your goodwill jar, and there's a chance when they come to you and ask for something next time, that jar will be empty, and you will say no. That's something they will have to learn, I guess. But you can't control their actions, as you know. Only yours.

When it comes to more serious things than dishes, I see this play out again and again. A wife gives and gives and gives to her husband who is happy to sit and be served. Then one day, she walks out with a suitcase, and he's left wondering what on earth happened. (I've seen this happen the other way around too!) Or maybe a brother helps and helps and helps his brother who just can't seem to get on his feet. Then one day, he doesn't answer the phone anymore. There is nothing left in the goodwill jar to give.

We have to make sure our jars are as full as you can get them, as much as you can manage. That's the thing about the goodwill jar. It's never done. Keep building people up and filling that jar every chance you get.

Give Them the Flowers Now

Growing up, I used to hear my parents and grandparents always say, "Give people the flowers now."

When we go to funerals, we always bring flowers in the culture I grew up in. It is a way to show love, but it's good to be reminded that it didn't do much good to the person who passed. They are dead, so they wouldn't ever know that you had brought them flowers. If you never gave them flowers or told them you loved them when they were here, what good is it now?

Well, it's the same thing in our relationships. People want to feel good now. This is how we make the world a little better all the time. Tell people how you feel, and give them the gifts in your heart. If somebody's doing something, celebrate them. It could be a friend, it could be a coworker, it could be anybody. Tell them in that moment and don't wait. Show your appreciation every chance you get.

We think that people know how we feel, but they don't unless we say it. This is especially true for our closest people—spouses, children, parents, and other very important people in our lives. We think that because we're around them all the time, they know we love them. But do you ever stop and think about how many times you are saying the actual words? "I love you." That's all it takes. For the way some people resist, you'd think it was an act of Congress or something. Don't be like that. Tell them how you feel.

Give them the flowers today.

Who Matters Most?

Before you can invest in relationships with anyone at work or in your community, you need to make sure your relationships with your closest people are strong and healthy. These are the most important relationships in your life.

My father used to always say to me, "Hey, son, in life you'd be lucky to have three friends who you can really call. Who come running, no matter how far away they are."

I didn't get it for the longest time, but I get it now. The older I got, the more I kept saying, "Dad's right."

If you think about it, you could say, "Oh, I have a friend who does this, and I have a friend who does that." It might seem like you have a lot of friends. But not really. You've got a lot of acquaintances. But are they really friends?

Let's say you're in a situation where you are struggling to financially make your mortgage note or whatever the case may be. Who's going to step in to say, "Don't worry. We got you till you get back on your feet"?

I think it's a good question to consider. If you were in real trouble, who would you call? Most of us will start with family. But be sure you're building that circle of people who can really help you during tough times because tough times are coming. I'm going to talk about this later in the book, but there will be times when you think, "Man, I'm in the valley right now, and I need a little help. Somebody lift me up so I can be strong." This is why I try very hard to surround myself with people who have the mental ability to help me move the needle forward when things are hard.

You know that law of physics we all learned in high school: like attracts like. When you surround yourself with people who have the same values and attitudes you have or want to have, you can't help but to fill up each other's jars.

But at the same time, we were also taught another law: opposites attract. It's good to seek out people who are different from you. I love it when my daughters bring their friends over. The energy is amazing! The younger generations are just incredible. It's OK to be the dumbest person in the room because that will lift you up to want to be a better you.

It's Not Always Easy

The goodwill jar is being kind to people even if they are really tough to get along with. Whether it's a tough neighbor, a tough coworker, a tough friend, a tough family member, or whatever. Especially in today's society with so many political and philosophical differences in relationships. There's a lot of animosity people have toward those who aren't exactly the same as them.

You know that certain people have certain views, so how do you maintain your self-control and try to build a relationship with someone who probably doesn't have the same values that you do? Or with someone who maybe doesn't look at things the same way you do?

The key is to find a common place. This is how you build meaningful relationships with your family, your neighbors, your coworkers, your boss, or your clients. This is where you really start building that brand I discussed in the last chapter. This is where your values set the bar of who you are.

People will either be drawn to you or turned away from you. The way you can fill that jar gives you a magnetic ability to draw people to you, making them want to be with you. In the workplace, supervisors will want to hire you and put you on their team. Coworkers will want to work with you, and employees will want to work for you.

But even when you are incredibly giving and patient and kind, there will be people who won't give back. You can fill their jar to overflowing as many times as you want, and all they do is drain yours. There have been times in my life when someone whom I had a really great relationship with made some comments that were pretty hurtful. Sometimes it was on purpose, and sometimes it wasn't. This is life. It happens to everyone.

So how do you handle it? How do you navigate through that?

Forgiveness is part of that goodwill jar. It is important to remember that everyone has peaks and valleys in life. It could be a health-related matter. It could be a marital issue. It could be a work-related problem. Whatever the reason, you can offer the benefit of the doubt and forgive.

It's really, really hard to do, I know. You won't forget a lot of time, but you can try to forgive people and move on. You never know, but you might be the one who should be asking for forgiveness first. Maybe you did or said something without realizing it, and you drained their jar first.

I do think it comes back to you when you do the right thing. Stacy Owens is an entrepreneur and consultant whom I highly respect. She said:

> I have learned the more I lift others, the more I rise. I believe with my whole heart the idea of elevation is not about you. The money comes, the opportunities come when you focus

on serving and helping others. When you experience the transformation of someone's life, you get to see it and you get to feel it. You get to hear it, and you get to touch it. It just all goes together. And still I rise!

We can all follow Stacy's example when we face adversity. We can lift others, and by so doing, we lift ourselves. Lifting to rise is something anyone can do.

Reflection Points

- If you had a self-report card for all the really important goodwill jars in your life, how do you grade yourself?

- Which of the goodwill jars in your life need your attention today?

- Who can you "lift" today as you go about your normal daily activities, and how can you raise them up?

CHAPTER 4

Relationship Dividends

In the strongest relationships, what you put in will always be less than you get out.

It seems like only yesterday when you were all bright-eyed and eager to please, but you realize that you are solidly into your career by now. You are meeting new, important people more often, and, in every relationship, you try to fill their goodwill jar. When you can remember to do that, you should admit. You have learned this is the key to promoting a reputation that best reflects who you are, but it's not always easy when there are so many demands on you.

You look up to a couple of your coworkers who are absolutely captivating, and you can't stop thinking about them. They embody the word "charisma," and it seems so effortless. Everyone wants to work with them, including you, but you can't quite put your finger on why. You are keen to crack the code so that you can be more like them.

You start to really watch what they do whenever you can. It isn't so much *what* they say; it's *how* they say it. Almost like their charm oozes out of their pores or something. How on earth can you copy that?

Investing in Relationships

The last chapter was all about the goodwill jar and how it works. I want to go a little deeper into why you should care about it. I want to use a little financial analogy to explain this. If I invest money in a company, the best result is that I will not only get my money back, but I will also get more money than I put in. That's the whole point of investing. When a company earns a profit, it can choose to reinvest the profits back into the business or distribute a portion of them to its shareholders in the form of dividends. Dividends are payments made by a corporation to its shareholders as a distribution of its profits. They are typically paid out in cash, but they can also be in the form of additional shares or other things of value. The amount paid to each shareholder is determined by the number of shares they own.

It's the same with human beings. In every relationship, there are dividends because we invest a little of ourselves—our time, our effort, our emotions, and our mental energy. What we get out of each relationship is the dividend, which sometimes is easy to predict and sometimes is not. Similar to the financial world, you put your investment in and hope for the best. Sometimes it works out, and sometimes it doesn't.

One of my very closest friends in the world is Eric Thornburg, current CEO of a major organization in America. A part of why we are so close is that we are evenly yoked. That means we lift one another up. When I'm down, he is there for me. When he's down, I'm there for him. That's what true friendship looks like. "As iron sharpens iron, so one man sharpens another."—Proverbs 27:17.

We've probably all had those experiences where it wasn't evenly matched. Maybe you gave a whole lot of yourself and got very little in return. Or maybe you didn't invest much of yourself, but you were blessed with an abundance of care and concern from the other person. Neither one is fair to either side.

It's important to recognize when things are not balanced. One of the questions at the end of the last chapter was about a personal report card. We were prompted to evaluate ourselves and learn to ask questions what kind of difference we are making in the lives of others in our fellow community members. How are we making the world a better place? Everything comes down to the way we invest in those day-to-day relationships with everyone in our lives.

I'm kind of a Tiger Woods fan because I see him as a master of his game. He is a world-renowned golfer and is considered one of the greatest in the world. I saw him on television once take time out of his tournament and walk over to a little kid who was holding a sign that said, "All I want to do is meet Tiger."

The kid was recovering from cancer, and Tiger, seeing the sign he was holding up, went over to him, signed the sign, handed him his golfing glove, and took a photo with him. Now, that kid's day is made. Tiger just took a few minutes to do something nice, and now that experience is going to stay with the boy the rest of his life!

None of us can be Tiger Woods, but we all have opportunities to take a few minutes out of our day to make someone else feel good.

Focus on the Good

We were in a restaurant one night with a couple from up the street for an early dinner. The server who came to our table looked exhausted. I asked her if she was OK.

"Yeah, I'm OK," she sighed. "Just got here, is all."

I said, "Well, look, we're going to be an easy table."

She said, "Thank God. I need an easy table today."

We all reassured her. "You're going to have enough tough tables today, so don't you worry about us. We're easy. Don't sweat us." You could tell she needed a break that day.

Shortly after that, she told us that someone before us had been really hard on her because their steak came out wrong. Sometimes it seems like we're all impatient human beings and we want everything right away. We think the world revolves around us, but it really doesn't.

We told the woman again that we were good. "We ain't got nowhere to go. If there are any more problems, we know you'll fix them."

We could see her relax, and it appeared her night went much better after that.

We all have a chance to do things like that every day. We could have been mad that she wasn't on her best game for us that night. We could have said, "I won't come in here again with my family!" But this place never has a problem. She just had an off-night, and that happens. We didn't worry about it.

Every day we are all presented chances like this. We can choose to not make such a big deal out of things, because honestly, most things really are not that big a deal. It's important to remember they are human beings. They're trying to take care of themselves the best they know how. This server, for example, was probably trying to take care of her family. We don't know what's going on in her life. Maybe she'd been working another job that morning or had been up all night with a sick kid. Try to show a little love and compassion.

I heard a story of the beloved children's television show host Mr. Rogers. His wife shared in his biography that he used to carry a piece of paper in his wallet with a quote from a social worker. "There isn't anyone you couldn't love once you've heard their story."

I really love that.

If you think about it, all of us want to be surrounded with a positive inspirational spirit like Mr. Rogers. You don't want to be with people who don't inspire your spirit for a better day. I mean, we've all had times when someone asks you to do something with them, and you really don't want to go because they are so hard to be around.

Imagine I'm someone who's always saying, "Let me tell you about everything that is bad in this world. The people who are bad and the situation that is bad."

You're going to think, "Jeez, this guy is wearing me out."

If a negative person like this asked you to dinner, maybe you'd want to just make up some excuse like, "I have a conflict this weekend." How many times have we all encountered this situation?

But remember, there's a difference between a person who has a bad day and a person who is a mental downer. It's good not to judge too quick. We're all going to have tough days sometimes, and it would be sad if that was what everyone judged us by. Sometimes we are down with sickness, health issues, or tough things with our loved ones.

And then there are those people who aren't happy unless they're miserable. They're a little trickier, but I believe everyone has light somewhere. Just like Mr. Rogers believed, I also believe you just have to look through the surface and find where it shines. And if you can't find the light in them, just move on. Make sure they're not in your inner circle. But really, I believe there's a light in most everyone.

Be the Right Kind of Cheerleader

For most of us, achievement in anything is really all about dreaming early and never giving up on your dreams. Think about all the people who worked for years to become sport athletes in football, basketball, hockey, or whatever the case may be. You have to dream before you can get where you want to go, or you'll just end up wandering in circles.

When I was young, I always dreamt of leading an organization and looking for something better. I worked with my dad in a landscape business while I was still in high school. We'd be out doing lawn care together, soaking wet with sweat, and I would stop and say, "Dad, I am going to have a house bigger than this."

He'd say, "OK, yeah. I know you probably will. But hey, right now, how about weed-eating that sidewalk?" (LOL!)

So, I was always dreaming, and while he didn't want to squash my dreams, he wanted to remind me that we had a job to get done.

I think it's the same for all of us. We like to dream big but have to remember that the best way to reach those dreams is through hard work. I always ask the young professionals I mentor, "What are you dreaming of? Are you thinking about where you want to be as you get older?"

I go in and talk to middle school and high school kids and ask the same thing. "What are you dreaming of?"

I love their answers. A lot of kids, especially young men, tell me they want to be an NBA basketball player or something like that. I pull up a little chart I have, and I say, "Guess what? Here is the percent of athletes, in almost every sport, who end up becoming going pro. Do you see that? It's less than 1 percent. So, if we had a thousand people in here, only one of you would get a chance. And even then, you might not make it." But I believe if you truly want to make it happen and put all the effort it takes, we all have the same chance to be in that 1 percent.

By saying this, it's not my goal to crush anyone's dreams. It's actually the opposite. I do this because it's good to dream realistically, especially at that age. They can still try for the NBA, but they are young enough that they have plenty of time to figure out what else they are going to dream about too. By grounding them in what is actually possible, I am lifting them up to dream bigger and better.

In 2023, brothers Jason and Travis Kelce made history by playing on opposing teams for the Super Bowl. Travis played for the Kansas City Chiefs, and Jason played for the Philadelphia Eagles. I was touched to hear an interview with their mom. Unsurprisingly, she said her boys had been dreaming about playing in the NFL all their lives. That kind of achievement is amazing but super rare. They clearly never gave up on their NFL dreams, but I'd be willing to bet, they had other dreams too.

Spread the Joy

Sometimes it seems like we live in a society where so much success is measured by all the wrong reasons. To make things worse, it seems like we love to beat up on people for every mistake they make. People love negativity.

I play a lot of golf now that I am retired, so I get to see how people behave when I'm out on the course. Golf brings out who we really are. It really does. Sometimes I see things that are a little embarrassing. These grown men have temper tantrums and throw their clubs around when things don't work out exactly like they want. (Those folks are not in my circles, by the way.)

Most of the people I play with aren't like that. If they are having a rough day, they might laugh and say, "Why am I hitting so many bad?" And that's it. I never throw my golf clubs because, to me, it's nice to just be out there in the sun. My first goal is to have fun with friends. Admittedly, I'm not that good at golf, so it's easy to relax and enjoy it. I kind of want to say to these angry guys, "You ain't that good either, so calm down!" They are always threatening to leave the course and never come back, but they never do.

I was talking to one of our pros at the pro shop, and he said all the members were complaining that the greens were too fast. "All these players keep saying the course needs to let the rough grow up. What do you think?"

I smiled at him and said I was all good. They didn't need to do anything different just for me.

He said, "Mr. Rowe, the problem is, you're about the only one who understands that. Because all us pros are thinking 'ain't none of y'all good enough to worry about how fast the greens are?'. But we don't say it because we don't want to create animosity with the members."

I don't complain about the greens. Generally, I don't complain about much of anything. If the golf course manager came and asked me specifically about the greens, I might say something like, "That green is really too hard for us amateurs." But he hasn't, so I keep that opinion to myself. Speaking out isn't going to spread any joy or cause any change for the better. The issues are already visible to the people who work there, so it's not my job to complain about anything.

With that said, if there really is something that needs to be brought to someone's attention, I will do it with love. I always try to bring a spirit of positivity when giving feedback to people I don't know. You see, I don't have anything in their goodwill jar yet because we just met, so I try to fill it up as fast as I can. I smile. I ask them about their day. I disarm them with love, just like I learned when I was a child during that math competition that I mentioned in chapter 1. (There go those foundation values again. You can't get away from them.)

None of us are perfect, after all. When you bring that positive energy, people will listen to you. It's the opposite of complaining. You just say, "Hey, would you mind if I give you a little feedback? Everything is going great, and you're doing a wonderful job. There's this one little thing I thought you might want to know about."

Usually, they'll say, "Hey, thanks for the feedback. That's a great point. We'll talk to the team about that and see what we can do."

This is how you inspire change while spreading joy.

There are even opportunities to bring positivity to the kids who clean people's golf clubs at the clubhouse too. Most of them are high schoolers or college kids trying to make extra money. I could be the guy who walks right past them to my car and throws my clubs in back because I don't want to have to tip them.

Or I can choose to be the guy who asks them to clean my clubs and then chats with them while we walk to my car. I can ask them about how many players they've seen that day. What are they studying in school? What year are they? How hard is that?

Then give them a little tip, it's not a big deal, but it fills up their goodwill jar. If we can all just take a little time to treat people right, imagine how much better things would be.

In the church, we refer to this as "pouring yourself into another." It's a metaphor for the time, energy, and emotional resources we freely give to others. It means you are giving them a deep level of care, support, and wholehearted commitment to their well-being and growth. Most people reserve this kind of relationship investment for only the people closest to them, but you can do it with anyone. Offer additional encouragement to everyone; make people feel special and valued.

Restaurants are the worst for this. People can be so rude to their servers. Servers can be so stressed. When they come to our table, my wife and I always try to disarm our servers right away with love so that they know it's going to be an easy table. Hey, how you doing? Been a busy day? My name is Nick. Boy, it's busy in here. I don't know how you guys do all this work and keep up with the pace. It looks so hard. I couldn't do what you do. I can tell you that. Can we start with just waters?

Now that person's already left with a good thought in their mind. But if I come in complaining from the start, that server is going to think, "Why'd you come here if you hated it so much? You know we don't force anyone to come in."

This is true anywhere you go. If you fly somewhere, thank the pilot and the crew. If you're at the library, tell the librarian what a terrific job they are doing. If you are checking out at a store, ask the person scanning your items how they are doing—and really mean it.

There was a time my friend, Brian Queen, and I had one of those opportunities to spread joy come to us. This is how he tells the story:

> I remember a time when Nick and I were playing golf together. There's a kid and his parents in front of us. The kid's probably about twelve, and so he's teeing off from the ladies' tees. We had never seen them before.
>
> The kid suddenly gets a hole in one right from the tee box. We saw it go in, and his parents started clapping. It would have been easy to just ignore it, but no. Nick runs up to the kid and congratulates him. He asks the parents if it's OK to reward the boy, and when they agree, Nick pulls out his wallet and starts counting out money. He hands it to the kid, all the time saying, "Good job, young man! You need to take this and go celebrate!"

> To Nick, that was very natural. He wasn't doing it to show off. It was just the genuine feeling of being excited for someone else and helping him feel like what he did was amazing. That kind of recognition of others' accomplishments, even a perfect stranger, is one of the most important qualities in a leader.

I had completely forgotten about that until Brian reminded me. But to this day, I can still feel the joy and enthusiasm of that moment. It would have been so easy for us to ignore it and just continue playing, but that would have deprived us all from something really special. When you fill the goodwill jar of others, you fill it for yourself even more. If we can all leave a little joy and spread a few sprinkles all the time, imagine the world we'd live in. This is how we can leave our world better than we found it. Our world needs a little more kindness.

You Before Me

While I was working on this book, I had a lot of conversations about the you before me philosophy. Often people find this really hard because humility is really spiritual. You have to be a humble servant first in order to put somebody else before yourself.

As we talk about the goodwill jar in our day-to-day interactions with our family and other loved ones, we give constructive feedback. Sometimes it's our spouse; sometimes it's our kids. It's important even though it hurts to give people hard and honest feedback. You're trying to get them to grow and develop, so hopefully they understand it's coming from love and not from a point of criticism. But it's a delicate balance. You have to make sure that everything you say is for their benefit before yours.

The you before me mentality comes in when you have to give constructive feedback to your coworkers, your subordinates, your superiors, or your clients. If you are living in a neighborhood, being honest is part of being a good neighbor. It's easy to get you neighbor's mail when they're gone or pull in their trash cans. There were times when I had the only snowblower, so I would blow off my neighbor's driveways. I did so because it's the right thing to do, so I wasn't keeping score, and I won't look for something in return.

But when you have an issue with your neighbor, such as maybe there's a property issue or somebody's ready to put in a new tree or fence, things aren't as easy. You want to make sure you don't offend them. These things can lead to disagreements, but if you got something in your goodwill jar, it kind of works out. They know everything's coming out of love, and they trust that you are putting them before yourself. So they know your heart was in the right place. They'll listen when you say, "Let's sit and talk about this thing rather than quit speaking each other for the next five years."

Thinking you before me helps in other circumstances. If a stranger is getting bashed, you can speak up. If you see a gossip circle starting, you can add comments of love and acceptance. Remind people not to judge before they understand the situation from the other perspective. Put themselves in the shoes of the people they are judging and resist closemindedness. Remember, gossip is easy. Love takes effort.

For leaders, this humble approach means you have to open up. You can say, "I'm the best leader in the world. If you don't believe me, just ask me." But everyone knows that's not the way it works. Your presence around people is what determines the type of leader you are. So take that shield down and be open enough to say, "You know, I'm just not very good at that." This helps your employees relax and trust you. This is the root of servant leadership.

Be vulnerable and show your weaknesses. Admit when you're wrong and apologize. Say those two hardest words—I'm sorry. And always admit when you make a mistake. Don't blame others. This fills goodwill jars.

Brian Queen is actually one of my past employees and currently the director of finance at a large organization. He is a big fan of the concept of the goodwill jar. I like that he combines it with the idea of being authentic in his life.

> I'm very much of a people pleaser, so I want to know that you think I'm doing a good job. You don't have to say much, for me to have to go above and beyond. I'll do everything I'm supposed to and then some. But even when you have people like me, it's important to build the relationships on things that are real. Leaders need to pour themselves into the people they work with, and results will happen. That's where authentic connection happens.
>
> Nick and I hit it off from the get-go. We have a lot in common, and we enjoy many of the same activities. When we were working together, people started to look at me differently because I was buddies with the boss. They thought I was getting special treatment, but it actually works the opposite. Nick was harder on me than anybody in the company. The fuller the goodwill jar is, the more you can ask of that person.

No matter what your title or station in life, when you live in accordance with your values, every time you are with another person, you can always add to their goodwill jar by putting their needs and wants before your own. When you go to your church or around your neighborhood or even at home with your family members, every day you make a deposit. Think before you start taking something out. We all leave a wake behind us, whether we mean to or not. You want wherever you've been to be a better place because you passed that way?

Don't Steal Others' Joy

My parents taught me not to steal others' joy when I was a child. I'm pretty sure they learned it from their parents. It is a part of the firm foundation that I was given. I know this isn't easy for some people. Small-minded folks tend to want to put everyone down so that they can feel bigger. I saw this happen once with my friend Sam Henry. I asked him if he remembered, and he shared this story:

> Nick was my strongest supporter and encouraged me to go to law school. To help me get ready to go, Nick took me to the mall to get some of the things I needed. We were just two guys shopping for appliances. I remember it so vividly, like it was yesterday. The guy at the counter was talking to us and asking me what I needed and why, and when I told him, he said, "You're going to law school? Oh, lawyers come a dime a dozen."
>
> Nick looks at the guy, and he looks at me. Then he says, "But here's the thing about that, Sam. If you don't make it, you can always come back here and sell appliances."
>
> That's the kind of defender he was of me. He had my back and supported me not only that way, but he supported me in everything I did.

I didn't do any more than what I've been talking about in this book. I put his feelings before my own. It would have been pretty easy to just ignore that guy and walk away, but Sam would have felt put down. I knew that being the right kind of cheerleader meant I needed to do something, so I chose to lift him in front of that salesman.

It works the other way around too. When people come to you and they are excited, let them have it. Maybe it's their first house, first car, first baby, whatever. So many times I have seen leaders take people's joy by saying something like, "I remember my first house," or "I was excited just like you when I bought my first Mercedes." That one-upping kind of talk robs people of their excitement.

This takes away the joy of the moment. Don't be a joy-stealer. Instead, give joy freely. Generosity will bring the joy. So does accepting the generosity of others. Let others do things for you. Don't insult them when they offer you their time, their money, their love. When you are generous, that can sometimes create an imbalance, so it is good to let others share their gifts.

In leadership roles, you have to be generous with your time and your grace. It's best to let others come to decisions on their own, even if you know a better way. They may get to the same place in their own way, and you don't have to make it about you and your way. You shouldn't rob that experience from them. And sometimes their way turns out to be better than what you thought it would. Figuring things out on our own brings joy.

With all that said, don't let anyone steal your joy either. People will try to tear you down, but you don't have to let them. There will always be those who are grumpy and say things like, "I hate Monday mornings. This is a terrible place to work." Or maybe at church they say, "I hated that sermon. The pastor needs to do better."

Don't let it pull you down. Avoid the lemon-suckers. They just will drag you down every time. And don't join in gossip ever. I risk being repetitive here, but gossip is just thinly veiled complaining. Professionals don't complain, so be a professional.

Be happy for those who stand a little taller. My daughter Ebony was Academic and Basketball All-American, but she never tells anyone that. You'll find her talking to young girls, encouraging them that they can make it big, not because she did but because she sincerely believes in them. I want to be more like her one day.

Can you leave this world today and be happy? I can sincerely say I can. Overall, it's been a pretty good ride. My advice to everyone is to live in the moment and not let anyone take your joy from you. As I get older, I realize I'm on the "back nine golf holes" of my life. I just don't know which hole I'm on because none of us do. But I do know I want to enjoy every stroke.

Reflection Points

- If you knew you were going to die tomorrow, which relationships would you most regret not building?

- Are there times when you wish you would've spread a little more joy?

- Who in your life could use a little extra light in their life today?

- Just like golf, what hole in your life are you on?

CHAPTER 5

Add Value

You are now at a phase of life where you are able to use your understanding of the goodwill jar with greater purpose. You continue to focus on strengthening the relationships in your life though, especially with people at work who are in positions of authority over you. After all, if you can be friends with the boss, that's a good thing. Right?

You don't realize it, but some of your superiors in management begin to notice how much emphasis you've been putting on building relationships. They start to get suspicious that you are forgetting what you were hired to do in the first place. And to be honest, you kind of are. Despite all of your careful networking, you are called into your boss's office one day.

You don't think anything of it. You two are pals, after all. It's probably just an invitation to grab lunch. How wrong you are. "Thank you for all you've done for the company," you are stunned to hear. "But we are going in another direction as an organization, and we need people who share the same vision."

You have been released from your position.

How can this be? You were your boss's friend! You were everyone's friend! You didn't do anything wrong!

But honestly, if you were to open your eyes a little wider, you'd realize you didn't really do anything *right* either. Sure, you built plenty of relationships and filled all those goodwill jars, but you didn't add value to your company. Being friendly can get you far in life but can never replace genuine hard work. Because of that, you failed.

What Adds Value?

Situations like the parable happen all the time in corporate America. It doesn't always mean that you have done anything wrong, but organizations change constantly, and sometimes your position is no longer needed.

However, sometimes it is because of you. You weren't adding enough value to your position for your superiors to justify keeping you. No matter what position, title, or level you reach in any organization, you have to add value through your responsibilities. It's fine to make and keep friends, but if you aren't bringing anything useful or new to your team, they won't need you for long. You will be replaced by someone who can add value or, sometimes, just a different value than what you have.

This scenario happens all the time. People are shocked when they are laid off, and they usually feel completely in the dark about why. If they are honest with themselves, it should be a wake-up call that despite the friendships they had, they still have to be nimble enough to adapt when things change.

This isn't just about the workplace—you must add value at home, while volunteering, at church, or anywhere else. It is up to you to show how much you can offer to make the lives of everyone around you a little better.

At the risk of sounding redundant, adding "value" just means finding ways to bring something "valuable" to those around you. It's not up to you to decide what they will find valuable. Instead, it's up to you to discover what they value, and then you need to figure out how to offer it. Adding value is about doing more than is expected without having to be asked to do so. It's also about asking yourself what could be valuable to other people around you and then actually doing just that.

There are opportunities to add value everywhere. Take on extra work to help a colleague, present a creative idea, or volunteer in your community.

If you want to be a great person, you have to first be a good person. Knowing how to add value is one of the key factors in going from good to great.

For example, does your family always disagree about whose turn it is to take the garbage out? If you just go and do it without making an issue of things, you're suddenly adding more value to your family because you're willingly filling a need. Better if you don't even have to be asked to take it out.

Or, maybe your friends never have a plan for how to spend the weekend, but they like to be together. You always come up with a few great ideas rather than falling into the "I don't know, what do you want to do?" cycle. Because of this, you are a valuable (and more desirable) friend to have around.

How about the workplace? Maybe you notice an inefficiency that has yet to be addressed, and you think of a solution. Then you quietly take the initiative to address the problem. I'd be willing to bet leadership will see that you are someone they can count on. When that happens, they will trust you more.

Everyone who knows me knows that I am a huge fan of my wife, Tyra. She is one of the most incredible people I have ever met, and I count myself among the luckiest men in the world to have been able to talk her into marrying me—and staying married to me since 1982.

She worked as a nurse for her entire career and was one of the most highly respected nurses in her hospital. She is a very humble person, but I pressed her a little for this book to find out what it was that she did to give her that distinction. This is what she said:

> I have been working since I was fourteen, and so I've always been a dependable, hard worker. I guess I never thought about it much. Growing up, I had a brother that was sick. He had sickle cell anemia. He passed when he was forty-two, but until then, he stayed in the hospital more than he was out of the hospital.
>
> I thought about my brother a lot and wanted to be the kind of nurse we wanted him to have. I guess that's why I went above and beyond. I just didn't come in for that paycheck. I treated my patients the way I wanted my brother to be treated. And I treated the families the way we wanted to be treated. I believe that's why I had a good reputation.

In fact, Tyra has had to be treated in the same facility she worked at with the nurses and doctors she worked with for years. She was a really good nurse, and so when she was on the receiving end, she was treated very well by the people she had developed relationships with during her career. It always comes back around.

She hits on a key part of this concept of adding value. It's the golden rule: treat others the way you want to be treated. And if you want to take it a step further, make sure you treat them the way they want to be treated. Everyone is different, after all. The things that I want and need aren't the same as the things you want and need. Adding value is about knowing the difference.

Adding Value

The principle of adding value is as important for organizations as it is for individuals. When a company can add value to the community, it won't go unnoticed. One example of this is Chick-fil-A, which is one of the most successful fast-food businesses in America for many reasons. One is that they are highly selective about who they allow to own and operate their franchises. It almost feels easier to get into Harvard than to open a new Chick-fil-A. But this doesn't keep people from being interested. According to *the Washington Post*, over 40,000 people begin the lengthy application process, knowing full well that 0.25 percent will be chosen.[1]

This fussiness pays off to the customers and communities because the new owners are massively committed to success, and they don't hire just anybody to work there. Owners only hire people who make each customer feel loved when they walk in the door. It's consistent in every single one of their restaurants, across the country. I could be in Texas or Kentucky or Indiana—regardless, I know the service is going to be good every time. I know that 99.99 percent of the time, my order's going to be correct, and the food will be good. Their app is easy to use. They can move people through a line. It's clear they train their employees to have a caring mindset. They bring your food to your car with care. When I go there, I am always impressed that they take the time to repeat my order to me to be sure I'm satisfied before I leave. That's adding value. Chick-fil-A has a crazy loyal fan base because they offer a value that you can't find in most other fast-food places, and because of this, their customers always come back.

---

1   Lydia DePillis, "It's Not Just the Pruitts: It's Really Hard to Get a Chick-fil-A Franchise," The Washington Post, June 7, 2018, accessed July 17, 2023, https://www.washingtonpost.com/news/business/wp/2018/06/07/its-not-just-the-pruitts-its-really-hard-to-get-a-chick-fil-a-franchise/.

I share this because you can be a Chick-fil-A kind of person—someone who strives for excellence and who has a way of making people feel that you care. That's a surefire way to add value everywhere you go.

I learned these lessons over many years of ups and downs. During my career, I worked for ten different CEOs in my last company. "Nick," many people have asked me, "How on earth did you survive that much turnover?"

My real answer was that I always felt that I was in the presence of the Master CEO, our Lord and Savior, Jesus Christ.

I realized it doesn't matter where you work or who you work for; you can always set yourself apart by adding value. As you create solid relationships, solve problems without being asked, consistently go above and beyond, and keep from being an obstacle to others, you will succeed.

Every executive has choices to make. They can hire or terminate anyone at any time. I tell my daughters, who are both professionals now, "Hey, look. You've got to be the most dynamic person there because when 'right-sizing' of an organization happens, your bosses are looking at keeping people who can get things done without a lot of drama. They will want people who show that they add value to the organization."

If you are trusted to do your job well without constant supervision, you have an advantage. Rather than being one to create chaos, you want to be one who brings a calming, happy attitude to work. Think of yourself as an ambassador for the organization you work for. People on the outside should be able to look at you and see someone whose work ethic and integrity are high. That is how you survive multiple bosses in your career, no matter where you work. Sounds simple, doesn't it?

The long and short of it: be easy to work with. It's OK to disagree, but don't be disagreeable. We will all disagree. That's how life is. Often that's how we come to the best solutions. But you must always find a good place of harmony so that everyone can move forward. Be on time. Outwork everyone else. Take pride in what you do. It cannot be about "you." Make it about "us." I love to see athletes in the National Collegiate Athletics Association's (NCAA) tournaments who win a game and say, "Hey, my teammates were prepared. They played a great game out there." They know that being a team player is key to adding value. And adding value is key to being a team player. You can't have one without the other.

The Danger of Complacency

I really love the quote by Rear Admiral Grace Hopper: "The most dangerous phrase in the English language is, 'We've always done it this way.'"

How true! We've all heard stories about the dangers of complacency, but I want to explore this topic a little because it is the opposite of adding value. Let's follow a business leader who gets lazy and watch what happens. This person builds a thriving company from scratch that comes to be known for its innovative products and exceptional customer service. Because of this, the company grows steadily over the years, and the employees begin to feel relaxed. The executive team stops actively seeking feedback, exploring new markets, and investing in research and development. Why bother when things are going so well? Everything is running smoothly, so there is no need for change.

As always, a rival company emerges, fueled by a group of ambitious entrepreneurs. This new company recognizes the changing needs of the market and quickly adapts to meet them. They embrace cutting-edge technologies that lead them to introduce innovative products and capture the attention of customers who are eager for something fresh and exciting.

You can guess what happens next because we see it all the time. The older company loses its established consumer base because it started taking for granted that a solid reputation will make up for their lack of effort. They forget that people gravitate toward novel designs and superior technology. The executive team of the old company stands, scratching their heads as their company collapses around them.

Complacency has a high cost in the long run. It's the same for individuals. A lack of motivation and a reluctance to challenge oneself lead to atrophy. When we don't learn from our mistakes, embrace change, and strive for continuous improvement, we don't offer as much to the world. We miss opportunities for growth and advancement because we settle for the status quo. Our creativity and innovation shrinks, and we lose our competitive edge.

The attitude that "good enough is good enough" deteriorates more than just our professional lives. It damages our relationships. When people become complacent in their personal lives, they fail to invest in the goodwill jar and become less attentive to the needs and concerns of those who are close to them. Over time, this can erode trust, weaken connections, and lead to relationship breakdowns. Those close to us feel taken for granted, which breeds resentment and anger. You cannot pour into others if no one has poured into you. An empty jar is an empty jar, so it is up to you to find ways to fill your own jar where you can.

I strongly encourage you to make sure you don't get lazy at home, in your performance at work, or with your own personal improvement goals. I like to pose the question, "Can you go to sleep every night knowing you put forth your very best effort that day?" If not, you might be getting a little too complacent. Now this doesn't mean to kill yourself overworking each day, but it does mean actually putting forth genuine effort. If you feel this is hitting a nerve, today is a good day to turn it around, beginning with the things you do on your own time.

When Nobody's Around

The University of California, Los Angeles (UCLA) basketball coach John Wooden famously said, "The true test of a [person's] character is what he does when no one is watching." True character comes out in the way we fill our time when nobody is watching. Ask yourself, "Am I true to my foundational values in every circumstance, even when I'm the only one who knows the choices I am faced with?"

Do you give into temptations when you know you can get away with things? Or are you an upstanding person, no matter what? Do you strive to make a positive impact, even if no one will ever know?

There's a slippery slope I've seen a hundred times. It can start in as simple a place as someone thinking that there's nothing wrong with taking a little longer lunch hour because nobody even notices when they come back into the office. They think it's no big deal. While that may be the case, they are sacrificing their integrity. Guess what? When you are leading, others are always watching.

You've got to be honest with yourself and others, and you've got to continue to work hard, no matter what circumstance you're in. If you take a longer lunch, make it up by staying later that day—even if nobody but you will notice. It's the honest thing to do. Don't take advantage of your employer.

I have noticed in life that when we start to justify our actions, that's a pretty good indication that we're doing something we shouldn't, and our conscience knows it. No matter how much we try to justify it, there is no right way to do the wrong thing.

If you find you are constantly explaining away or justifying your choices, even if it's just silently to yourself, pay attention. These are the times to tune into the voices from your foundation. I often hear my parents, who have passed, still whispering in my ear. It's probably same for you. They are whispering to you for a reason, reminding you what's right and what's wrong.

It might seem like it doesn't matter logically. After all, what's a few minutes lost here or there? But trust me. It matters. Your actions behind closed doors are an indication of your honor, your character, and your values. You can be the kind of person who wouldn't eat a grape in a grocery store without paying for it first.

I'm not perfect by any means, but I do feel a sense of satisfaction knowing I always dedicated a full day's work for a full day's wages. I was paid in full every two weeks on payday, and then the clock would start again.

Get Results

What does value mean in terms of an organization and its employees? I mean, all that soft stuff that we have talked about so far sounds good, but guess what? It doesn't help if you can't get results. After all, that's what they're paying you for. You have to execute, or you won't be around. Through your career, you have the opportunity to be one of those people who gets things done. Or not. You can be one who always accepts new tasks and training. Or not. This will be a part of your brand.

There's a common saying in the business world: if you want something done, find the busiest person and give it to them.

It sounds kind of counterproductive, I know. But it's true. If you sit in or visit a barbershop, you can always pick out the best barbers because they have a line in front of their chair. Even if there are three other barbers sitting there with no customers, the best ones will be in the highest demand because people know the quality they offer. Be that person whom people can rely on.

Remember that made-up "you" at the start of the chapter who suddenly got laid off? The day before it happened, they were feeling cozy and comfortable, thinking, "Well, my bosses seem to really like me. They won't ever let me go because I'm special."

But believe me, if they can let you go and still get the work done, you're not necessary. It's only a matter of time before you're replaced, and they will be just fine after you leave because you never actually did the work or added value.

Someone told me once that they heard an economics professor say, "You can drop me in any town in America with only the clothes on my back and a quarter, and I'll be fine because I know how to add value."

(I think this must have been a long time ago, when a quarter was actually useful to make phone calls. I guess today you'd have to substitute the quarter for a phone!)

I like this story, because by the end of my career, I agreed with that professor. I was never afraid of getting fired, because I had figured out how to get the results I was hired to get while still building relationships. That was my way of adding value.

It doesn't matter how many close relationships you have if you can't produce results. That's the danger of servant leadership sometimes. You have to be careful not to get lost in your focus on building relationships that you forget to still add value. Sure, you can do the right thing and inspire people, but don't forget that you have to produce results in the job you were hired to do. At the end of the day, it doesn't matter if you're a grocery store clerk or a CEO. You've got to actually do the work.

Don't Take Advantage

When people are treated fairly, they are usually more likely to treat others fairly too. When I was an executive, there were many times when we would be looking at a candidate and knew we could pay them a lot less than what their predecessor was paid because of where they were relocating from, or sometimes even because of what they felt they were worth.

I would tell the other executives, "I understand this candidate adds a lot of great value regardless of what they have been paid in their previous position, so I want to make sure we fairly compensate for that."

The flip side was true as well. I didn't want to ever be paid more than I was worth. I have always appreciated people who did not feel they were owed anything more than what they had earned. A sense of entitlement is one of the worst things an employee can have, in my opinion. How often have we all seen people working for a family member and never actually doing anything? Or people who have been a part of an organization so long that they don't actually work anymore? They think, "My value is me. I'm so important, they can't do anything without me." Or, "I'm only a year from retirement, so what the heck? What are they going to do? Fire me?"

Just because you may have a personal relationship or friendship with your boss or coworkers, you should never ever use that to your benefit. Never take advantage of people whom you work with or of your friends and family members.

My wife and I have a long list of friends we enjoy sharing dinner with. There are a few who I know will always pick up the check every time. But that's not right. I have to race them with my credit card to make sure we are paying our fair share or pick up the check entirely. Of course, I could sit back and say, "Hey, man, you guys are great. Thank you for taking us out!"

They'd never say anything about it. But where is my integrity then?

I have always been inspired by people who give more than they take. The world needs more givers and less takers. I'm not just talking about money. Rather than taking advantage, they give freely of their time and their love to make sure you know you are cared for. These are the people who are thoughtful in everything they do. They know how to love in a truly Christlike way; they are the people who will sorrow with those who sorrow. They pray for you when you need it—not in just the "thoughts and prayers" way that you always hear—and they really make an effort to lift you up in your time of need. They are the people who text you at just the right moment to let you know you aren't alone. They can't help but to overfill your goodwill jar every time you are with them.

This is the kind of person I try to be. Sure, I fall short sometimes. But it's my goal to leave this earth being remembered for being a giver. You never have to quit caring for people.

Be Yourself

In the end, the best way to add value to the world is to be your authentic self. One of the people I respect most for being able to bring something truly valuable to every relationship is my friend Eric Thornburg. I was curious why this skill came so naturally to him, and so I asked him. He said, "I grew up playing soccer in high school and college. I had many teammates, all with different backgrounds and ethnicities. As a result of that and my own upbringing, I was always comfortable with people who were different from me."

I was impressed by that. It all comes back to our foundation and the way we learn to build relationships in the early years of our lives, doesn't it? Because Eric was raised to see the value of everyone around him, no matter what they looked like or where they lived, his children did too. He went on:

> We lived next door to Nick and his family at the beginning of
> our careers and became close friends. I distinctly remember
> vacationing together down in North Carolina one year and
> realizing how wonderful it was that we could enjoy each

other when our children were very young. My daughter Erica had very blonde hair and green eyes, and Nick's daughter Ebony had a dark complexion and black hair.

Watching the two of them walking down the beach together, holding hands and playing, warmed my heart. I saw everybody on the beach look at them and be encouraged by it. They'd start racing each other down the beach, and I could see the impact that had on all the people for good. I thought about it then and vividly remember it that it was kind of an example for how Nick and I could serve together. Who cares about our differences? We're friends, and that's all that mattered. It was a beautiful moment.

I have seen this same thing play out so many times. People who have the skill of adding value from a young age tend to be completely unaware of what they are doing. It comes so naturally. I have seen it time and again in my career. And I have always tried to help bring that out in people when they don't realize they have it.

I can remember when we recommended Ashli Watts to the Kentucky Chamber of Commerce Board of Directors as one of the youngest executives nationally. We recommended her because we knew she could offer a tremendous amount of value to the organization. She didn't know this about herself at the start, so I did my best to help her see that all she needed to do was be herself, and everything would flow from there. When I asked her about that experience for this book, she shared:

Leaders need to show empathy to today's workforce and support them. Nick never made me feel like I had to be something that I wasn't. I could be a thirty-seven-year-old mother of two and still be a state chamber president and do a good job. (I think some women don't have that type of support. But where Nick has two very successful daughters and a very strong wife, he's always been a strong supporter of women.) He knew that I could do things that, at that point, I didn't think I could do. Just knowing someone believed in me gave me the foundation to let go of trying to be something I wasn't, and to just do the job I knew I could do.

And she has done an incredible job ever since.

Don't worry if you weren't raised the way Eric or Ashli were or if the things you just read about in this chapter don't come naturally to you. Thank the Lord it is a skill that can be learned. You can follow those foundational values that make your brand authentically you as you add value to the lives of everyone you meet. It starts with the smallest of efforts. Smile at the busy clerk at the store. Wave and say hello to your mail delivery person.

Then look for ways to make meaningful contributions that might take a little more effort. Mow your neighbor's lawn when they aren't home. Build a Little Free Library in your yard. Be the person your coworkers can come to when they need a friend. Make your boss look good. When you commit to doing something, make sure you follow through.

Rather than thinking, "How can I add value?" (which might not come naturally), think, "What can I do today to make the world a little better?"

You have to have a will to win, the ability to stay focused on the job at hand, and the fortitude to ignore the outside noise before it gets in your head. Don't lose your confidence. If you do this consistently, you will become the most valuable person possible, because you'll see the options for adding value are endless!

Reflection Points

- Who are some of the most valuable people in your life?

- What do they do that makes them so special to you?

- What are things that you have noticed other people complain about lately?

- What are ways you can help relieve them?

- When you are with your boss, do you give credit to your employees and take responsibility for failures?

CHAPTER 6

There'd Be Days like This

After everything you've done to build strong relationships, you feel betrayed and discouraged because you were let go by a job you thought you were good at. You half-heartedly search for new positions on the internet, but those searches quickly slide into mindless hours of scrolling through social media. You can't help but to think of all the ways you have failed in your life. Even though this is the first time you have been released from a position like this, you are noticing a pattern. You realize that this isn't the first time you have been shocked by people telling you that your performance was lacking.

In fact, it seems like every time you think things are going along just fine, you get knocked down. Every time you've been evaluated, the same comments keep coming up, but you blew them off. Up until now, it's been easy to dismiss and explain it away as "their" problem (whoever "they" were). You thought you were doing so great professionally, and now you are sitting in your pajamas on the couch every day. Is there a lesson you are supposed to learn here?

If there is, you're too depressed to figure it out. You can't figure out where you went wrong. Where do you even go from here? Are you going to have to move back in with your parents?

Peaks and Valleys

When you're going through life, you're going to have peaks and valleys. No one is going to have a perfect, event-free life. There will always be challenges, no matter what. That's just the cycle of life. When you're on the top of your game, you can expect that there will be some storms on the horizon. Now this doesn't mean you should live in fear of all the possible bad outcomes. Especially in the good moments. Enjoy them and make the most of them. Just be prepared to endure the inevitable valleys of this life.

It's sort of like a good sermon at church. A pastor always says, "Hey, you may not need this today, but put it in your goodie bag because you're going to need it."

Maybe right now, you're on the top of the mountain today and everything's great. But then you go to one doctor's appointment or get one call, and it changes everything in a moment. It could be a new challenge at work or the illness of a loved one that makes your world crash. We have all been in those places where you feel like you lost a part of your life.

It's good to pay attention to the times when we are on the mountain or in the valley. If you're on a mountain right now, that's great! Take advantage of that time to fill up those goodwill jars and contribute and add value because you know there will be valleys ahead. That's just life. We can't get lazy during the good times because we'll need to have something in the tank when the challenges come.

When we're in a valley, we wonder why everything is so bad. Why isn't the road smooth? What did we do to deserve this? Where do we belong? And, more importantly, how can we get back on top again?

The way we face our challenges when we're in the valleys determines our forward trajectory in the workplace, in our relationships, and with ourselves. We have to meet the trials that come at us by falling back on our basic values. I believe when similar challenges arise over and over, it can be a sign that you have lost track of a part of your core identity, your foundation. Sometimes the source can be hard to pinpoint, but until you break from that, the cycle will continue. We can't let our guard down on our values.

I always say God hits you with the small hammer until he has to get out the sledgehammer. He keeps coming to you, trying to teach you the lessons you need to learn. And then you are finally like, "OK, I got it!"

You finally have to admit that maybe the problem ain't some fictitious "them." It's you. The good news is, God covers us in good and bad times with His grace and mercy.

Tough Feedback

One of the hardest but most beneficial things we all must do is to hear tough feedback. It comes in just about every aspect of our lives. Neighbors, friends, family, and coworkers all have the right to tell you when you are doing something that doesn't work for them. Whether they do it tactfully and constructively or not, it doesn't matter. Each of us has the responsibility to learn how to take tough feedback well.

If you've never had a 360-degree evaluation at work, brace yourself. It's a performance assessment where you get a full circle review with your superiors, peers, and direct reports. They are given an extensive questionnaire and anonymously score you. They all rate your strengths, weaknesses, behaviors, and competencies. It's a snapshot in time, a cross section of the way you are perceived professionally.

It really breaks you down mentally. Narcissists tear them up and throw them away. We all want to get the highest scores, but you never do. It's an experience that will dump you off the deep end of tough feedback. It can be a real eye-opener. We all want to be the best at everything we do. And we usually think we are. But really, we're imperfect. Every single one of us. We've all made mistakes, and hearing about them from people you work with is hard, and it hurts.

The first time I had a 360 review, I was like, "Dang! I work pretty hard, and I try to do all the right things, but people are saying this about me? I can't believe it."

I read things like, "You're too impatient" and "You take too long to make tough decisions."

When everybody knows you have a problem but you, that hurts. I realized I wasn't as good as I thought I was. It didn't mean I was a bad person but that, just like everyone, I was imperfect.

It's good to try to take a deep breath and return to the conversation later, because your natural action is to get your wall up, right? No matter what it is. Try to give yourself space to reflect on it. Don't get defensive. And don't dwell on it. Take the negative feedback as an opportunity to learn things about yourself you aren't always able to see.

If you go by what people say to you all the time, and let that dominate your whole life, you'll never get out of the storm. To this day, some of the feedback I got is still hurtful, but I had to make a choice. I could have said, "Gosh, I have to get out of here. Poor me." But I didn't. Instead, I took my first 360 as an opportunity to show I belonged in that position. I deserved to be there. I decided to make a more conscious effort to work harder and to educate myself. I looked for ways to improve my value to the organization.

If you let them steal your joy, you'll have a much harder time moving forward past it. That first 360 evaluation experience helped me grow and develop personally and professionally. If you have had a similar one in your life, how was it? If you've had two, how did you deal with it the second time? Hopefully, by the third time, you can navigate a little better.

You always have a choice whether to accept the feedback or not and to make changes based on what you have learned. It's not just what we do that matters most; it's how we handle ourselves when times are tough that makes a leader a leader. As so many people say, how many dead bodies are left on the battlefield as you charged the hill and took the mountain? This is your chance to see if you're alone at the top.

It doesn't matter where the feedback comes from—whether it's your spouse, kids, neighbors, friends, coworkers, or bosses—it can be painful. It's the subtle things that people do and say to communicate their frustration or anger with you. We are often a product of our upbringing, and things that hurt back then still hurt today. Don't let that trigger you. You can waste your time fighting over one hurtful comment. You can give into anger and plan your revenge, sucking your time and talents into an unproductive realm.

Or you can rise above it, move on, and leave the negativity behind you. Remember, don't let them steal your joy. If you want to dwell on it for hours and hours and even days, all it will do is rip you apart. As leaders, we have to move on. People are inspired by our actions, and they watch what we do.

It's a constant balance. It's being able to say, "Hey, OK, that was a pretty tough comment you made, and I am hurt by it, but I am going to turn that around." Hopefully you can get that person to understand how their comments or actions hurt while giving them the benefit of the doubt that maybe they didn't realize what they were doing. Or maybe they're struggling with something personally, so pointing out the faults of others is their way to hide from themselves. Regardless, dwelling on it is never good. It helps to try and just move on. But don't be so fast to move on until you ask yourself why that feedback came to you in the first place.

We all have to take accountability and ownership of our words and actions. I always suggest that the first thing to do when you get a comment that seems hurtful is to try and see if there is any truth behind it. Be willing to accept that sometimes maybe you are at least partially at fault. Try to see it from their perspective. We have to be careful, because anything we do or say may be hurtful to someone else. We all have said and done things to people that we wish we had not. We wish we could take them back, but we can't. We forget that a careless comment may impact them the rest of their lives. We may think it's not a big deal, but to them, it is crushing.

I always try to listen a little more deeply when I feel like I am being criticized. I think, "Well, maybe what they're saying is partly true, so I need to do a better job of explaining myself and maybe they would have a little different view."

Take responsibility instead of making excuses. We all make decisions, and there are always consequences for our actions. Even in the most casual of settings. What might happen if you join in the fun instead of sitting on your phone? You could be someone who brings positivity to the whole group. Maybe the feedback you are getting is just a nudge to help you meet your potential.

The next time you get feedback that seems hurtful, take a minute to step back and get curious. Look for the silver lining, the golden nugget in the words that can help you boost your performance and strengthen your relationships. That is the most productive thing you can possibly do—working to learn the lesson, so God doesn't have to pull out that sledgehammer.

Boundaries

Have you ever met those people who seem to have just one challenge after another, all the time, almost as if they attract particularly bad things? Then there are those who seem to have the opposite. They see blessing after blessing. If you look closely, sometimes you can pick up patterns there. People who are constantly trying to fill up the goodwill jar of others and leave places better than they found them tend to have more positive things happen. Call it karma. Call it "what goes around comes around." Whatever you want. But it's true. The way you treat people is the way they treat you.

You'd think this would be common sense, but sometimes people are just not nice. They are bigoted, racist, sexist, ageist, or whatever. No matter how hard you work to find the grain of truth and address their concerns constructively, there will always be negative people who drag you down.

When these challenging people come into your circles, don't spend time wishing they would just leave. Rather, the first thing to do is try and be that person who inspires. Be that person others want to be around. You can always choose to befriend them and show love to them despite their difficult personalities or your natural instincts to steer clear.

Our whole world centers around whom we hang around with. Expand your circles. There will be times when you are coming down off that mountain and headed into the valley when you will need all the friends you can get, so don't be so quick to cut people out of your life. Even if they seem to be a bit negative, maybe you will need their realism in the future.

Sure, maybe you don't want to go to dinner with people you don't have much in common with or play golf with people who are negative and who are taking the joy. It's normal to think, "That would be the most painful four hours of my life." But do it anyway. My wife and I always tried to make sure we were leaving a place better than we found it. Every time we moved, we'd find a way to contribute and be positive so that when we left, we would be missed for all the right reasons.

You don't want to be the kind of person who walks out of a room and people say, "I'm so glad they left."

But this doesn't mean you have to be best friends with everyone. My dad used to say to me, "You know, you'll be lucky to have three true friends by the end of your life."

I'd say, "Dad, I've got a thousand friends."

But he'd continue to say, "Those are acquaintances. You'll be lucky if you have three."

I get it now. True friends aren't the same as the thousands of friends we all think we have. Ask yourself, who can you really call if things are bad? Who, besides family, will come running, no matter how far away they are, day or night? Who will help you pay your bills if you were struggling financially, and say, "Don't worry about it. I'll help you get on your feet"? Who will stay by your side, no matter what happens?

That circle is pretty small. My parents had so much wisdom, which I only realize more and more as I get older.

So, we have that tiny handful of people who are true friends and a (hopefully) large group of people who are normal friends. But then there are always a few people who are drains to us. Energy vampires, as they say. How do you set boundaries with those people so that they don't constantly drag you down? How do you exit those relationships, which is not easy to do?

My daughters, Dominique and Ebony, have a list of "Dad-isms" that they laugh at now. But one of them has stuck with them both. "Your yes-es are just as strong as your no-s." You can say no to fifteen things, and that means your yes is going to be even more powerful. It will reflect who you are and what you believe is worth giving your energy to.

To determine this, I think the first rule is to stay focused on your foundational values, your integrity, and your character. You establish boundaries by your actions. People will know by watching how you interact with others what kinds of things you will and won't tolerate.

I like to let people know I'm an imperfect person who makes a lot of mistakes, but I'm a man of faith. They can see in my behavior that I don't tolerate any kind of behavior that is against my standards. I'm devoted to my spouse and my kids. Without me having to say anything, people notice I'm not going to say or do certain things. They usually pick up the hint that if they want a friend who does, they have to look somewhere else.

But if they don't get the hint, sometimes you have to be honest about what is happening and make the choice to have a hard conversation. "Hey, no hard feelings, but that's not the kind of person I am. It's not that you're wrong or that I'm wrong. It's just that I have different views on things. My values don't align with yours." It is important to find those who share your values because they lift you up, reinforce your goals, and keep you accountable to the standards you share.

Most people don't take that approach because it can be really uncomfortable. I've had to do it quite a bit in the workplace with people who were my peers. I had to explain to them, "We're not evenly yoked, so it's best if we don't try to force it. I always try to surround myself with people who have similar values as me. It doesn't mean that my values are perfect or right, but that's who I am."

I find there is a middle ground between these two approaches, which I guess you could call a soft exit. You just don't let them into your circle anymore. When they ask you to meet them for lunch, or to attend an event with you, you just always say, "Look, I'm busy."

If you do that enough, they usually drift off and find other people to be their friends. Through that process, you kind of eliminate the negative people in your life. It's not that this is easy. There have been plenty of times where I was the odd man out because I didn't want to spend time with certain people. But I never let it get to me too much. I've always been comfortable in my own skin and never really wanted anything from anybody, so that's helped.

Personally, I've always kind of just spoken my mind and been pretty transparent, and, thankfully, it's always worked. I've always kind of used that as a barometer. If I'm honest with myself and others, then I'm OK. Sure, I'm imperfect with my own challenges, so I don't expect anyone to be perfect either. But I try to find like-minded people to bring into my closest circles.

I know it's cliché, but I find honesty, really, is the best policy. It just makes life very simple when you keep it so clean. Like Dr. Martin Luther King said, "Our lives begin to end the day we become silent about things that matter."

That last part is key. There absolutely are times when you have to challenge people. But there are other times that you might not need to make a big deal over things that don't really matter. Let's say you're on a plane sitting next to someone who says something slightly offensive. You don't want to make a big confrontation with someone you'll never see again. I guess that's a judgment call we all make.

Personally, I'm not going to argue or debate about something that doesn't really matter. As a Black man, there have been so many times where racial issues have come up in my life. Nobody wants to talk about race because it scares everybody. I believe most people are worried to say the wrong thing, so my default is to give people the benefit of the doubt. Things might get said differently than they intended. It happens to all of us. But there have been a handful of times when I knew that it was intentional, and those were instances where I had to draw the line. There are certain things nobody should tolerate.

I think we all have the opportunity to decide for ourselves where we want to build relationships and where we need to be willing to lose them. You put your anchor down in the waters where it matters most to you.

I once had a particularly challenging time in my career that was public enough for people in the community to form opinions. My wife was working full-time in the hospital, and in light of the public discourse, one of her coworkers had some particularly strong and negative feelings about me. She would make remarks all the time, even when my wife was in the room. Finally Tyra had enough:

> Normally, you can just walk away from that kind of thing, but after a while you get tired. It just took a toll. It's taxing every time you turn around.
>
> I finally just said, "I'm really tired of hearing that."
>
> She said, "What are you talking about?"
>
> "You know what I'm talking about," I said to her. "I don't want to hear it again. I've always been a believer that everyone's entitled their own opinion, whether I like it or not. And you are wanting me to hear what you have to say. OK. I'm letting you know I hear you. Now hear me. I don't want to hear it again."
>
> I never heard it again.

I love this story, and I am so proud of her for the way she handled it. She didn't destroy the relationship or get hateful. That would have made the work environment very tense for a long time. Instead, she was respectful and requested respect in return, and in the end, her coworker got the message.

I mentioned earlier that Tyra and I decided that in every community we lived, we were going to leave it better than when we first got there. Imagine if everybody had that sort of mindset! Just think how great this country would be! That's all you need to do.

Humble, Vulnerable, and Faithful

As we age, our confidence should grow exponentially. But we all get to that point where we realize how much we don't know. It's fun to watch as young adults get shocked at the realization that their parents are actually pretty smart! Teenagers think they know everything until they start to live on their own and see all the other people out there who know so much more. It's an important, humbling experience.

All that advice we get as young people starts to hit home especially when we are struggling with challenges we have never faced before. Building relationships in these circumstances means letting your guard down and being vulnerable. So many people put a shield up when they are down. It's particularly important to be vulnerable if you are in a position of leadership or authority over others. Be humble enough to admit what you are going through and ask for help. This is the mark of a true leader.

Imagine the power of having every leader, parent, teacher, and friend be able to say to those near them, "I'm having a hard time here because I'm not very good at that. Have you ever had that same situation? What did you do to get through it?"

That's the beginning of servant leadership. Knowing there is value in every person, no matter how young or old they are. We can let people know we have the same hurdles that they have. That's part of creating goodwill, admitting when we're wrong.

I can remember so many times as CEO when we'd have a team meeting where everybody shared their thoughts. I'd make a decision after I took everybody's feedback, and then it wouldn't be six months later, and I'd have to come to them and say, "Hey, everyone, you guys told me to go left, but I went right, and I was wrong. I screwed up. Help me get us back on track."

And every time, it was OK. My team would understand and help me through my mistake. Part of leadership is making decisions with the facts that you have and doing the best you can. But we all fail sometimes. In those instances, honesty, vulnerability, and faith will help weather the storms. When repeated similar challenges arise, it can be a sign that you have lost track of a part of your core identity, your foundation.

It helps to remember that there is a Master CEO who is really in charge here. My faith in God has always given me a long-term perspective so that I can navigate the hardships. It helps me to stay positive, stay focused, and work on healing when the deepest wounds are cut.

I believe God tests our faith. He really tests our faith in the valleys. It seems like the closer we get to God, the more challenges we have sometimes.

Anybody can have faith in good times. It's so hard to have faith when things are not going right. Do you keep your faith, or do you forget it when you're in those low times? This is a clear indication of your core values at work.

Learn and Move On

History repeats itself. This is another phrase that is extremely overused, but I think that's for a reason. We're going to keep making the same mistakes until we decide to learn from them. This is a fact of life. You know the old "definition of insanity," I'm guessing. It's doing the same thing over and over, expecting different results.

I've made plenty of errors in my life. From financial errors or mistakes in external affairs or the way I dealt with the public or media, there were times it felt like I couldn't do anything right. But what I could do was try to keep from making the same mistakes twice. I expected the same thing from the people who worked for me. In my industry, we have critical safety measures that must be followed, and when a mistake is made, it can have life or death consequences. My team always talked about the safety near misses and how crucial it was not to repeat them. My biggest responsibility was to get people back home the way they came to work.

As I write this, it's that time of year to change the smoke detector batteries. I've got that on my list to do. Last time I did this, I got the wrong ladder from the garage, and it was not tall enough. Instead of going to the garage again to get the right one, I just stood up on my tiptoes on the top of the short one. Talk about a near miss. I could have easily fallen and broken my leg or arm.

I kept thinking about my dad, working with him in the land-scaping company. At that time, we all had our electric mowers. I can hear my dad saying to me, "Keep the cord behind you. Keep the cord behind you."

If you put the cord in front, you are probably going to cut the cord. I always did what he said and never once ran over my own cord with a lawn mower.

The near misses can sometimes be as important as the mistakes. This time when I go to change my smoke detector battery, if I get the wrong ladder again, I will listen to my father's voice. I will learn from my near miss. It's going to take a little bit longer, but it's safer.

Despite our best efforts, things never go perfectly. I try to set an example when things go wrong that became an unofficial policy:

1. Own what you've done. Don't blame anybody else.
2. Learn what you can so you won't do it again.
3. Move on.

I used this same pattern at home. Another one of my "Dad-isms" that I used to always say to my girls when they were growing up is, "Anybody can make excuses. You can always find ten reasons why you can't do something, but if you can give me one reason why you can, then you should be able to do it."

Dominique told me:

I used to hate that because if I came home with a bad grade or something, and I made an excuse, Dad would be like, "Well is there a reason you could have done it?" And I would usually find a reason. It used to make me mad, but as I got older, I realized that it was really good. The default is to not make excuses. Your default is to find a way to do what you have to do, even if you know it's going to be rough. Even now I think, "How I can make it happen?"

I would always tell my daughters, "Learn what you need to learn, and consider it another arrow in your quiver. Another tool in your toolbox. And move on."

I also believe that when you find meaning in what you do, that gives you strength to get through the challenges that might come. My friend and colleague Susan Lancho is senior manager of External and Government Affairs with her organization. She has some wise words about this topic:

When you face challenges in your career, it's important that you don't lose your character. I would say dig deep to make the most of the situation you're in, but know that it's OK to look for other options it that's best. If you're consistently not happy, you're going to take that home, and who wants that? Why spend the majority of your week doing something that's not life-giving? I was in a position at one point that wasn't life-giving for me. I could do the job just fine, and I could make a living, but that's not how I wanted to spend my time. I discovered that I needed more, so I knew I had to make a change.

I wanted something to feed me a little more than just the paycheck and the benefits. Of course, I'm appreciative of those, but I needed more fulfilling work. When that happens, still do your best work and stay true to who you are in terms of being a positive, productive employee as you navigate through your next steps. I guarantee you'll still learn from the experience. You'll learn what you want and what you don't want from your next position.

I have found that I don't mind hard work and putting in the extra hours when I enjoy what I do and when I find real meaning and purpose in it. Find what you are passionate about and that will carry you through any challenges that come.

It doesn't help to dwell on the negative. People are always watching, and that reputation that you build lasts a lot longer than the embarrassment over a mistake or two. Be humble enough to take correction when you screw up, or if it doesn't come, be wise enough to give it to yourself.

Better Times Ahead

How do you take the challenges that come and find a little good?

I find that it's helpful to look backward and see how far you've come. Seeing what you've already been through and overcome can inspire you to keep striving and dreaming big dreams.

One of my favorite professional memories was the day I was able to ring the closing bell on Wall Street. The executive team of my company was invited to come to the floor of the New York Stock Exchange. It's just like you think—ticker tape everywhere and people running all over. And there I was on television at four o'clock, and everyone was clapping. I'm just a country boy from Bowling Green, Kentucky. Who would have imagined I would ever be in that position? It was the summation of my career. I knew that everything I had done was represented in that moment, and it was so much bigger than me. It was about God's grace and mercy in my life. I wished my mom and dad and siblings could have been there to see it.

What if I had gotten distracted as a young engineer and just kept my head down? Or if I had held grudges every time I was slighted and sat in my cubicle full of anger and regret? I never would have had this opportunity to experience this amazing moment. Instead, I am grateful I had the right mentors and influences to help me learn how to set myself apart at work. There were plenty of chances to let the hardships get me down. I remember specifically a time when I was very new in my career as a young engineer, and some money had gone missing from one of my coworker's drawers. The police were called in to investigate. I was working at my desk when one of the officers pointed at me and said to his partner, "Do you think it's him?"

I was doing exactly what everybody was doing that day, but I was the only Black person there. I hadn't even thought of that until that moment. Thankfully, my colleagues spoke up and defended me, and I chose to let it go. But this sort of thing happens to people all the time, whether we are discriminated against, harassed, abused, or neglected. Nobody is guaranteed a life free of challenges.

Our choices in the hard times can kill our dreams. We can see them as growing opportunities or as crippling hardships. We can choose to build the mental strength from them or to let them get the best of us.

I'm on the back nine of my life right now. I don't know if I will get to play a full eighteen holes or not, but that's OK. I look back on the picture of me and my team on Wall Street and think about where all those people are now. Some of them went on to bigger things. Some of them have passed on. You never know where you're going to be next, so enjoy the moment that you're in. Even if it's just this ordinary, mundane, routine normal day. There is still joy and amazing beauty in that mundane, normal day, right?

Reflection Points

- How do you take the challenges that people give you and make a little good out of even the toughest trials?

- How do you keep from making excuses and instead take the negative and turn it into something that can make the word a little bit better?

- How do you know when you need to set a boundary with someone?

- What does that process look like?

- Can you think of a time you received negative feedback? How did you react, and what might you do differently next time?

CHAPTER 7

Save the Best for First

You have weathered the storms and landed a new job. You're finding that it is so much better than your last job, something you never thought would happen. You love the work. You love your team. You even love the office itself. Every day you work up feeling energized and excited to go to work. You find yourself going in earlier and staying later than you really need to. But why not? It fulfills you in ways you didn't know a job could.

To make matters even better, your kids seem to be doing fine now that they are growing up a little more. You are busy with volunteer activities every weekend with the community and the church. To top it off, you're finally asked to serve on a board, something you've been hoping to do for a long time.

Everything is going along beautifully now that you're back on top of the mountain again. This is, until the day you get home, and your spouse is standing at the door with a suitcase. "I need to take some time away from you to think about our relationship." And out the door they go.

You are blindsided. You find yourself confused and left wondering, "What on earth is going on?"

You sit at the kitchen table in a quiet house, wondering how this could happen. Haven't you been doing everything you needed to do? You paid all the bills. You came home every night. Granted, sometimes everyone was asleep by the time you got there. And you missed a few of the kids' games and concerts. Well, maybe more than a few. What activities are they in again?

Do you even know what grade they are in this year? And your spouse. When was the last time you had an actual conversation about more than the calendar or what to eat?

And here you thought you had it all. Are you really being asked to choose between your work and your family?

In the quiet, you start to reflect on all the subtle (and not so subtle) signs that things were going downhill at home. The comments your spouse and kids made. The hints that your close friends gave you about work-life balance. And the way your boss looked at you with a hint of concern when everyone except you left their desks at the end of the day. Even on Fridays.

If you're honest with yourself, you know you were wishing that you didn't have all the demands at home that you had. In your heart, you were quietly praying that your family would lay off the guilt trips and leave you alone. Well, guess what? They did.

First Things First: Keep the Faith

Just like the story presented here, people have moments in their lives when they have to recon with themselves and what they really value in life. I have to put faith first here because it's the order I live my life. People tease me sometimes that I can't complete a single conversation without giving praise to God. Even in formal meetings and speeches, my faith is in my blood. And I am unapologetic about it.

God is first, and everything else comes after. My family lives our lives to do what God wants us to do before we do anything else. I know that God always has a plan for me and my family. He pushes us to be better than we were. He supports us in our trials. My hope in Christ is that there is a better place for us. I don't want to go there any time sooner than I have to, but when I do go, I hope I'm ready to answer that trumpet call and be held accountable for my life here on earth.

Maybe you aren't a believer in God, the way I have been using that term. Maybe you have a different faith system entirely, and that's fine. But research has proven again and again that having faith in something bigger than oneself has given human beings the ability to be more content, resilient, and hopeful. Philosophers have explored the significance of this, as having faith provides a framework for understanding the world and a guide to living a meaningful, ethical life. Practitioners in the field of psychology recognized it as an important component of emotional and mental well-being, as it promotes greater resilience. Faith-based organizations and community leaders often emphasize their role in fostering social cohesion, moral values, and social responsibility. Faith motivates people to engage in acts of charity, service, and altruism in ways that few other causes do.

God usually gives us exactly what we wish for. Just like the character mentioned in the story who wanted to be left alone, God gives us what we want. Sometimes we think the grass is greener, as they say. He'll not only show you that grass is not always greener, but He'll also make sure you see exactly what blessings you had before you wished them away.

It's my preference to live in humble gratitude for what He gives me and let Him decide if I need anything else. I would rather pray for the benefit of others than to bother Him with my petty requests. He takes such good care of his children when we allow Him to.

I asked my friend and colleague, chief global officer of a large corporation, Valoria Armstrong, if she had any thoughts about faith. She is a massively talented and accomplished woman, but I have always respected the way she has lived her faith in all aspects of her life. She humbled me with her memories of the time we worked together. She said:

> I think any kind of leadership role that you're in, you have to stay true to who you are as a leader and the values that you have. I always knew where Nick stood in regard to his foundation. It was God and it was family. Then work came after that. He didn't put anything before his spiritual beliefs, his Christianity, and his family. He was so proud and continues to be so proud of his daughters. We always knew what was happening in their lives. His wife, Tyra, is such a calming spirit. She is a caring, loving woman. I think she and Nick really balance each other so well. Corporate America is hard, but being in the (municipal) water industry is a tough space. There is a lot of pull on you. We all knew what Nick stood for all the way up to the last day of retirement.

It goes back to what I said in the last chapter. When you live your values, people notice. And more than that, those who share those values are drawn to you.

If you are struggling in your faith, I highly recommend taking some time to search your heart and find your higher power. Find a community of believers to be with, and let them help you develop the kind of faith that will stay with you for the rest of your life. That's a journey you won't complete in this life, but it's one you will never regret.

I understand that there are some people who are confused about how to live their faith in the workplace. My friend Traci Cross is the senior director of Operations in her organization. I love her thoughts about living your faith in the workplace:

> The three hundred people that I have working for me most likely all know I'm a God-fearing person. They know that because I interject it in ways that are subtle. I'm not going to push my beliefs on anyone, but I think it's important for them to understand my principles and the reasons I do what I do. When I hear other people talk, I listen and then I might subtly add something about my own faith. Then I wait to see if there's an avenue or invitation to take that any further in our conversations. And if there isn't, I don't push. But if there is, it can be a good way to build relationships.

If you are a person of faith, any faith, you can live your values without compromising your professionalism. It doesn't have to be one or the other. Let your values guide the way you build your relationships, and you can't go wrong.

#FamilyOverEverything

There was a time in my life when I had the choice of family or work presented to me. It wasn't by my sweet wife, thank heaven. It was from my young daughter. I had been given a job opportunity that seemed like a really good thing for me professionally, but it required our family to relocate. We had everything in our car, and we were driving down the road to our new home.

From the back seat, Ebony, who was probably six at the time, said, "I don't want to move. I love my friends."

"You're going to have friends there," my wife and I reassured her.

"But, Dad, what about school? Don't we love our school?" she asked.

"Yes, but you'll have a good school there too," I said.

"What about your job, Dad? Don't you love your job?" she persisted.

"Yes. I did love my job," I agreed.

"Then why are we leaving?"

My wife and I looked at each other and realized that we really did have everything we needed back where we were living. We prayed about it after listening to Ebony's sincere and innocent comments. The next morning, I declined the new position.

Sometimes decisions are that easy.

It gives me a sense of humble satisfaction to hear my wife and kids talk to other people about our family. "There was never a time where we knew family wasn't the priority over everything else," I heard Dominique say to her friend once. "He's very cool and chill, and everybody likes him, but when it comes to family, he plays zero games. If anyone interferes with us, they're going to have a problem."

My daughters can tell you that I never missed a single one of their games (and there were hundreds!), concerts, recitals, or school programs. Even if I had to stand up and walk out in the middle of a board meeting to take their calls, I would. As they became more and more accomplished, it grew more and more complicated to be at all of their events. We had to buy plane tickets and get hotel rooms to see them play in college, and I never once regretted a penny I spent for that. In the end, what else would I spend my money on that was more important?

Did it hurt my career? Maybe a little. I'll never know. But I don't care. It didn't hurt me any more than my regrets would have hurt me as a father. Because I put them first, I have memories with my girls that nobody can take away from me. That is more valuable than any other compensation I would've received by staying in the office.

I see so many people take the opposite approach. They never take time off work to go to their family's events; they send their spouse with a phone to record it all. That's their own career decision, and it's not up to me to judge. But it's not my style.

We use the #FamilyOverEverything tagline as our family motto. And now that we are growing in number—both girls are now married—there's even more love to share. I love bragging on my new sons-in-law and supporting them both in their lives. They are learning that my wife and I are their biggest cheerleaders. We can also be their toughest critics, but that's only because we love them. We expect great things out of our children because they are great people.

I enjoy watching my girls as they volunteer with children now. Ebony is a basketball coach for kids in her community, and she told me once how interesting it is for her to watch how other parents are with their kids. "Some of these parents are just delusional with their kids and their abilities. I am so glad my parents were always real with us. They supported us, but they didn't coddle us. If I was upset about a game, my dad would say, 'Well, work on it. Do better. Go put in the extra hours.' That shaped me into who I am today, and I'm proud of what I was able to do."

As parents, we always supported our daughters, but we were always honest with them. Our success is measured by how much will we leave "in" our daughters versus how much will we leave "to" them. What we really want is to leave their hearts so full that they can continue to be good people long after we're gone. That will stay with them forever.

Strength in Marriage

Marriage has become almost disposable to some people, but it doesn't need to be. It can be the source of one's greatest fulfillment, strength, and joy. Tyra and I have had plenty of ups and down in raising our children and having busy careers, but we have never once questioned our commitment to each other. One of the reasons we have been able to stay together so happily for so long is that we continue to date each other. Just because we're empty nesters and retired doesn't mean the romance should end. I still get her flowers, and she still makes my favorite dishes. We treat our relationship like a full-time job. There's always a give-and-take when two people are together for this long. We work every day to fill up each other's goodwill jar, and every effort is worth it.

If you are married, ask yourself how many things you actually do together. Do you go grocery shopping together? Do you share the household responsibilities? Do you take time to actually talk each day?

My friend Eric Thornburg has been married to his amazing wife, Melissa, since 1983. He said:

> Nick and I approach our marriages in a similar way. Our wives are both amazing women who had their own careers. My wife was a schoolteacher, and Tyra was in nursing. They both set their careers aside while we were moving and transferring and raising our families. Nick and I both looked at our responsibilities as husbands to serve our wives and serve our families, so they understood how much we appreciated and respected what they were doing. They were staying home with the kids, raising them, and being the backstop for our families while we were running around, going to meetings, traveling, and investing in the careers. What our wives were doing was really more important eternally than what we were doing.

It's important that you keep a personal humility about whatever your partner choses to do. Nick's retired, and I'm pretty close. At this stage, you realize life moves pretty fast. Marriage is all about communication and putting each other first. If I work for my wife's success, and she works for my success, that's beautiful. It's not easy. I mean, it sounds easy, straightforward, and simple, but it's not. We all have our own selfish moments. But if you want to go the long term, this is the only way that really works.

Marriage isn't 50/50. It can't be. In fact, you shouldn't bother trying to keep score. Sometimes it needs to be 80/20 or 90/10. It doesn't matter. The strongest relationships are those where both parties are fully committed 100/100. Both of you are all in. I like to ask myself, "Have I filled my wife's goodwill jar full enough that she will change my diaper when I'm old?"

Work-Life Balance

Who owns your work-life balance? You do.

My job has always been third priority after God and my family. The idea of being careful what you pray for is very important here. If you desire that C-Suite office, you just might get it. But are you prepared for the sacrifices that come with that job description? Will it give you the flexibility you require to be the spouse, parent, and friend you want to be? Will it force you to make tough decisions that you aren't yet prepared to make? Everyone has to make that conscious decision.

You might get more money and more professional respect, but you lose other things. The intangibles that you can't put a number on, such as devotion and love at home, memories of your children, and time with your aging parents.

I know so many managers who wanted a position at all costs, to the point where they gave up everything to move all over the country. We all know people like that. They sometimes forget that their professional goals may cost them their family. You have to figure out what's best for you and your family.

Sometimes the best thing is to just be thankful for what you have. Of course, you don't want to be afraid to venture out and take on new opportunities, but you have to know what you're getting into. You have to see the whole big picture.

For me, decisions like these were easy: faith, family, job. In that order. It might be different for you, and that's OK. Your job may come first. Or your family. There's nothing wrong with that. Just know what you're giving up when you put one over the other. Therein lies the balance that we try to strike.

Some things only come once in a lifetime. Be careful to make sure if you are going to miss those things, it's for something more important. We're only passing this way one time, after all. You can't go back after you retire and say, "Well, I think I'd like to go to my children's parent-teacher conferences now." That ship sailed.

I was always a little saddened when I would hear people brag about how many vacation days they had left at the end of the year. Like it was something to be proud of. How many special memories could they have made with their young family by taking those days for a vacation? How many important bonding moments did they miss because they were so focused on not taking those days off? You don't get those moments back.

With that said, it always makes me laugh when my girls reminisce on the family vacations we did take. The things that are meaningful to kids aren't always the things you think. They'll remember fondly the "cool" rest stop where you stopped for a break and have no memory of the amazing beachfront property you rented. Or they'll talk about the one taco they ate and forget the rest of the lavish trip you gave them. Or worse, they'll talk about the time you got food poisoning, and everyone had to leave you in the hotel throwing up while they went to the theme park—and somehow that is their favorite memory! Kids are so funny that way. You don't get to choose what matters to them. And in the end, it doesn't matter what they remember specifically, as long as it is a memory of the family being together. More good comes from that than anything else.

Take your vacation now. Work hard, but play harder. I don't think it's anything to brag about to retire with a perfect attendance record ("I had perfect attendance for 35 years!") if you have a family. If you are getting pressure to sacrifice your family for your job, get a backbone and say, "Hell, no." You have every right to put your people first!

Let's not forget your responsibilities that we discussed in earlier chapters about adding value. You can add value and still have a work-life balance.

Friends

Having strong social connections with friends is also a hugely important part of life. They provide a source of emotional support and companionship. Sometimes you need someone who isn't family, to listen, offer advice, and support you in your troubles. Human beings are social creatures, and having a network of friends can fulfill the innate need for belonging.

I know adults tend to think they don't need friends, but studies have shown that strong social connections are linked to better physical and mental health. It's true!

Friends can help you have different perspectives, which increases personal growth, critical thinking, and empathy. Therapists say that pain shared is pain halved. It literally cuts that suffering in half when you can share the burden with someone else. Keeping your priorities in the right place should give you the ability to be there for those you care about most in their times of need. Being there means praying for people when they hurt. It is listening, supporting, talking, giving advice when it is asked for, and shutting up when it is not. It's knowing their limits and yours.

My daughters are closer than any two sisters I have ever seen. I know they talk every day, sometimes multiple times a day, and they make a habit of checking in with each other before they unload their stresses. "I need to talk about something. Are you in the mental space to hear it right now?"

And if the other one isn't, they'll say, "Life is lifeing."

That's code for, "Not now. I love you but I can't handle your crap, because I have my own crap right now." It doesn't mean they don't love each other just as strong as ever. It just means they both know, as empathetic people who feel heavy, just like their parents, they have to be careful. As servant-oriented, giving people, the act of listening can sometimes be very draining.

I choose to see friends as a gift from God. We weren't put on this earth to be alone, so why on earth should we isolate ourselves? A life well lived is a life well connected.

Reflection Points

- What are your top three priorities in life?

- What are you doing to make sure you are keeping them in that order?

- What might you need to change to keep those priorities better?

CHAPTER 8

Someone Has to Do It

Solidly mid-career now, all your hard work is really paying off. You're in upper management at your company, which is great for the compensation and benefits. Unfortunately, it also means you have to lead evaluations, conduct assessments, and make some really hard decisions as your company grows. You have to fire someone you really like, something you haven't ever had to do before.

You remember the time you were fired by that manager you thought was your friend. All these years, and you still have a sore spot over that. But now that you are in their shoes, you start to feel compassion. As you look at the reality of what needs to be done for the good of the company, you suddenly see that old boss through new eyes. You really don't want to fire anyone, but this person doesn't fit the organization anymore. This must have been how your boss felt about you all those years ago.

Because of how betrayed you felt and the hurt you've carried all these years, you are extra motivated to handle this delicately. The two of you have worked together for a long time. You are even close enough to have an idea of how their finances are, and it's not great. They have young kids, student loans, and a mortgage. The whole family is really going to suffer. How can you do this?

But your boss keeps telling you that the company is only as good as its people. Nobody prepared you for this. Is being a leader really all it's cracked up to be?

You're Only as Good as Your People

So much pressure is placed on leaders to make sure they are selecting the "right" people for their teams. I hear people say, "Make sure you have the right people in the right seats at the right time." Leaders have to consider this with every new hire, transfer, and promotion they make. But what makes a person "right" for a position? And once you know that, how do you find those "right" people?

One of the more prominent elements in this conversation is diversity, particularly in big companies. For me, diversity is like fishing. You throw the net out into the sea to see what's out there. You pull the net in, and if you're lucky, it's full of fish.

You reach into the net, and you say, "Boy, that's a good-looking fish. That's the best-looking fish there." It just happens to be a big green fish. That's OK. You like that fish, so you keep it.

Then you pick the next one, and it happens to be a sleek, striped fish. Well, that's a great fish as well, so you keep it too. And the next time you might keep another one just like it. Or you'll keep three little polka-dotted ones. The point is to keep the very best fish in the net.

I always think of diversity in hiring like this. If you only pick people who look like you and think like you, then you don't get the diversity of thoughts, ideas, actions, and processes. People who are different from you will always have something different and valuable to offer. It's not about fishing until you find one specific kind of fish that looks a certain way. It's about casting as wide a net as you can and then choosing the best from all of them.

To me, it really is that simple. You're just trying to do the right thing. You get good candidates, and you get bad ones. There's nothing wrong with that. As a leader, don't hire the bad ones, even if they fit your organization's view of diversity. If you do, you'll end up having to find a way to get rid of them.

That said, be careful not to judge anyone based off someone who looked like them in the past. I was talking to an executive recently who had hired a person to fulfill their idea of diversity. He said, "Well, we hired a Black lady to work at the front desk years ago, and it didn't work out. So, we aren't going to hire another one."

I laughed out loud at him and said, "Well, how many white males have you hired that didn't work out? A lot, right?"

He looked at me, surprised. "Well, yeah."

"So, it's no different."

He said, "Wow, I never thought of it like that."

You've probably heard the saying, "If you've met one [fill in the blank], you've met them all." This is ridiculous—and so is what that leader implied about his Black employee. It's like saying if you've met one person named James, you've met them all. Or if you've met a person with curly hair, you've met them all.

See how silly it is to generalize an entire group of people based off our interactions with someone else? If you've met one doctor, you've met one doctor. Not all of them. If you've met one child with autism, you've met one child with autism. If you've met one Vietnam War veteran, you've met one Vietnam War veteran. You get the point. Be careful about judging based on preconceived notions. It's never fair to project personalities, experiences, attitudes, and skills onto others.

With that said, I understand the pressure to make your best guess when trying to hire the right people. The last thing you want to do as a leader is to put yourself in the position to have to terminate or displace someone you just brought on. I always tell leaders, don't rush your decision. If there is a vacancy, I know you want to fill it right away, but it's worth to cast that net as wide as you possibly can. Gather all the fish in the sea so that you can find the very best one for that opening. It might hurt to have that vacancy open longer, but I promise it will hurt much worse to have it filled quickly by the wrong candidate.

Partnering with the right person is hard. There's only so much you can know of someone from an interview. It's always a risk during the hiring process. It's easy to pass over someone who is too sloppy, too casual, or too egotistical. No-brainer, right?

But then there are also the candidates who give you their very best in the interview, and you don't know that it's all an act. This has happened to every executive I know, including myself. We are super impressed with the applicant based on their strong resume and interview. They say all the right things and ask all the right questions. We bring them onboard, with high expectations.

And then they crash and burn.

Once I hired a guy who interviewed really well, only to find out he couldn't build a relationship to save his life. Within weeks, I had to go back and find a way to exit him. I felt embarrassed, frustrated, and irritated that I had to start all over. It's kind of like dating someone for an hour and then deciding whether you want to marry them. The honeymoon can only last so long.

So how do you get the right person? Well, I'm sorry to tell you I don't have the answer. But I do know it helps if you can look past their qualifications. I know that's the first thing we all look at, especially if we're hiring positions like engineer, attorney, or accountant. If they're very qualified, we think they'll be a good fit. But you have to look beyond those factors too. Look at their attitude. Can they get along with people? Can they build a team concept? What's their emotional intelligence quotient (EQ)? Do they align with your company values? What kind of relationships did they leave behind in their last position, and why did they leave, for real? Are they humble and teachable?

If people have the right attitude, I believe you can teach them pretty much anything. But if they think they know everything already, you probably aren't going to be able to change their attitude.

I love the quote by British journalist Miles Kington: "Knowledge is knowing that a tomato is a fruit; wisdom is not putting it in a fruit salad."

Do as much research as you can with the permitted questions. Call those references and past managers. Pay attention to your instincts. Of course, you don't want to discriminate, but you do want to be very wise about who you invite to be on your team. You are as strong as your weakest link, after all. Don't be the one to bring on another weak link.

Making Those Hard Calls

Every leader has times when they must make changes to their organization. Sometimes it's as simple as making new policies or creating new safety guidelines. Sometimes it's rolling out a new IT system or accounting process. These are relatively easy.

Other times, you have to be the "bad guy" and give people tough feedback. Of course, people like to hear all the good things that they are doing, so giving praise is easy. In my experience, very few people want to hear how they can improve. That's human nature, right? It doesn't matter where it's coming from—our spouse, kids, coworkers, or superiors. Constructive feedback can be very hard to take, and can even be hurtful, despite how it is delivered.

When I was in a position where I knew I had to tell an employee something that might not go over well, it helped to remember when I got reviewed by my superiors. Remember that 360 evaluation I got? I try to put myself back in that frame of mind.

Sure, someone has to do it, but do it with love. Be kind. Keep those goodwill jars as full as you can so that there's something left after. The Bible talks about clipping the vines. Any seasoned gardener knows that you have to prune sometimes to help a plant to grow healthy and strong. When they get overgrown, they put their energy toward things that don't bear fruit, such as growing more leaves or getting taller. If you're trying to get a good harvest, you need that tree or bush or vine to put its energy toward the fruit instead. Giving constructive feedback can be like clipping the vines.

People often have a hard time understanding why we are hard on them, especially when they think we're giving negative feedback. A teenager might think his parents are being mean when they tell him that he needs to fix his attitude and get better grades. He doesn't want to hear it. But every parent knows these hard comments come from a place of love. We want to help our children grow even if that means they need to be trimmed a little. We're hardest on the ones we care about most and those who have untapped potential.

Having a hard conversation with employees is kind of like being a parent. The reason you're hard on them is because you love them. You don't do it because you're trying to be mean; it's because you know what they are capable of. I've had to say, "You know we appreciate all you do. You've been with us for eight years. But guess what? You've got to step it up. You've got to find a way to get this done. It's your job, and I know you can do it."

Sometime love is hard. We can't wrap children in cotton balls and bubble wrap and expect them to get strong. They have to fall down and scrape their knees sometimes in order to learn how to walk. Loving parents sit near them as they struggle and suffer a little, and then when the time is right, they coach from the sidelines to help their children avoid making bigger mistakes later on, when the stakes are higher. Having those hard conversations with integrity and love often leads the employee to learn how to be leaders themselves. You'll see how they begin to adopt your leadership style as time goes on. It can be not only very inspiring but also very humbling.

Remember how I talked about the way we don't get to decide what our children remember fondly from a family vacation? The same principle applies here. We don't get to pick what our employees choose to learn from us. We do the best we can and hope that they get something positive out of it. We can only hope employees take the positive attributes from us and leave behind those things that we don't do so well, as imperfect leaders.

I do caution leaders of one thing, though. Don't expect too much of a change right away. After all, you chose to hire them, and you chose to keep them. Again, it's kind of like a marriage. I tell my wife, "After all these years, you know all my warts and I know all of yours. If we think we're going to change each other now, we're wrong. But we can change together."

There are times when a hard conversation isn't enough. You do everything you can to try and light a fire in the underperformers. You offer all the training on relationships and team building to the introverts. You take the struggling ones under your wing. And it's still not enough.

Sometimes you have to swallow your pride and admit that you made a mistake and hired (or kept) the wrong person. The higher a person goes in leadership, the more this happens. You have to know how to exit certain players on your team when it becomes clear that they are not working out. If you do it the right way, it can make all the difference in the world to that person, to you, and to your whole organization.

Don't get me wrong—firing someone is never easy, but there is definitely a good, better, and best way to do it. If you've never had to terminate anyone, it's very, very uncomfortable. I always said when it became easy for me to fire people, I shouldn't be a manager anymore. If I was that callous that it didn't hurt, that meant it was time for me to quit. It never gets easy. It's always very physically, emotionally, and mentally draining. You don't sleep well for weeks when you know it's coming. You don't eat well. You can't concentrate because you constantly ask yourself, "Is there any way around this? Have I given them every opportunity?"

But in the end, you must look out for the best interests of your entire organization. You have to make sure you have the right people in the right seats at the right time. Firing someone is a surefire way to drain their goodwill jar empty. Hopefully it will have been full enough beforehand that they won't hate you forever, but there's no way to control that. Your only choice is to take a deep breath and do it.

Early in my career, most of the bosses I knew were old school. A manager would fire someone and then brag about it to everybody. "I kicked his butt out." As if it was something to be proud of. The tougher you were, the more you cussed and shouted, the more powerful leader you were.

I never bought into that. I always thought to myself, "OK, look! I've got to terminate this person, but I know they are a good person. They may not be a good fit for us, but they could be a good fit somewhere. I need to do this with dignity and respect."

Leaders can always be courteous and handle firing someone without embarrassment when giving an explanation to the remaining team members. Sometimes less is more in these cases. Something like, "They are a good person, and we're so glad we were able to have them while we did. Now they are taking advantage of the opportunity to go a different direction in their career."

Ashli Watts learned this so well when she took over the role as Kentucky State Chamber of Commerce president and CEO. She came in to lead an existing team and knew right away she had to make some tough changes.

> Leaders have to do hard things sometimes, like letting people go. It's important that you have support around you. I always think about this question: Who do you want to be in a foxhole with when you're in battle? You want to be with someone who is strategic, action oriented, and compassionate.
>
> I moved into a position where my predecessor was very beloved. There was a shift from a sixty-six-year-old man who'd been there for fourteen years to a thirty-seven-year-old woman. Though I wanted to be a caring, compassionate supervisor, I also wanted to set very high expectations and a culture of excellence and of performance. You need someone who has been there to bounce ideas off of or just kind of vent to sometimes.
>
> It helped that I'm pretty action oriented, just like Nick, so I relied on him. He was always there if I had questions. It never seemed like a nuisance to him when I had to call and report on what we were doing or ask a question. He taught me a very good lesson that I now quote to my staff almost daily: "Don't come to me with a problem unless you have a solution."

> When problems would arise, he would say, "Well, what are the possible solutions? Let's go through the pros and the cons of each of those possible solutions, and eventually we'll figure out the best path."

In my career, I had to exit someone who had been with the company for many years due to some ethical issues that had come to my attention. Because of their history with us, I really wanted to do it the right way. I wanted to give this person the chance to say that he decided to retire, which would have allowed him to keep his dignity and respect. Some people on the executive team were against that process because it would take a little bit longer.

But I fought for his right to leave with his head held high, and it worked. People thought he retired, so he kept his dignity and even heard comments on his way out like, "Lucky you. I wish I could leave at your age."

Nobody knew he really didn't want to leave. And in my opinion, that was the least we could do after he had devoted so much to the business for so long. I wasn't interested in being tough. I wanted to be fair and kind.

In the end, as a leader you are the one with the long-term, big-picture perspective, so you ultimately know what is best. Sometimes you have to make sacrifices to keep your company healthy. The best thing you can do is start from a place of gratitude for everything an exiting employee has done to this point.

Servant Leadership

Coming from a place of love is central to servant leadership. Leaders have to get results; we all know this. But to do so, you don't have to lose your values as a person or your knowledge of what matters most.

The challenge of servant leadership is to build strong, value-added teams that deliver results and are the kind of teams that make up for your inevitable weaknesses.

Servant leadership is a lifestyle, not a temporary choice. The "you before me" philosophy can continue long past retirement if you choose to let it.

My friend Bruce Hauk is currently the COO of a large organization. He is one of those people who seems to really embody this philosophy. When I asked him to share a few thoughts, he said:

It is important for leaders to be involved in the work of their teams, but not to a point that they risk missing the big picture of what is important. This is where you find the courage to say what needs to be said versus holding back and letting things continue to run afoul.

Being a servant leader is foundational to our spiritual backbone. The importance of serving others versus serving yourself and not losing ground to your principles or your values, regardless of whether it's meeting numbers or not. How do you bring yourself to help others? I think from a servant leadership standpoint, it begins with asking yourself how much are you willing to invest in your teammates and to build those relationships? That creates trust, and then the trust allows people to be vulnerable. Many times in the competitive business environment, nobody wants to seem like they have any challenges, concerns, or struggles because it may make them appear to be weak. That ultimately stymies trust development and team building.

Nick fostered and created an environment where we knew we all had challenges and struggles. Everyone knew we could talk in confidence and trust we had each other's best interest in mind. My goal as a leader was to help people see that I wanted to try to help as much as I could with positive intent.

Trust is built over time and through intentional actions and investments in others. In my career, I have had some very deep conversations with team members about what those challenges were and what to do about them. You have to trust the relationship by offering sensitive issues that matter to you as well. When you give a little trust and see it not betrayed, you gain more and more confidence in those relationships.

During the time I worked with Bruce, sometimes I would visit with the various operation districts and speak to our workforce that oftentimes was unionized. I remember Bruce sharing some frustration with me over some of the labor relation challenges we were having. They were arguing over the provision of coffee cups, T-shirts, and other seemingly trivial things—kind of missing the big picture of what we needed to talk about.

I had to remind the managers how important it is to know what employees need versus thinking we always know what their priorities should be. Sometimes you have to appreciate walking in their shoes. The quickest way for someone in a leadership position to understand what their employees are asking for is to put themselves in their same situation.

If someone asked, for example, for rubber boots or gloves and the leader is resisting it and asking for justification, I would say, "Well, go stick that leader down in the same hole where his people are working and allow him to work there for a little while."

The leader will pretty quickly understand why they need boots and gloves. Sometimes we'll lose a dollar to save a nickel arguing over these kinds of things. That's just part of being nurturing to your people. Are you willing to walk in their shoes, experience what they experience, appreciate their needs, and act on it?

Being a servant leader means you strive to find the good in all people, even if they are not a good fit for your company in that moment. It is about prioritizing the well-being, growth, and success of your people before yourself.

In order to do this, you have to actively seek to understand and meet their needs by having empathy, compassion, and a willingness to listen. Instead of controlling or micromanaging, a servant leader empowers team members, providing them with the necessary tools, resources, and support to succeed. They focus on developing the skills, talents, and potential of others. Servant leaders prioritize building meaningful relationships based on trust, respect, and collaboration. They foster open communication and encourage diverse perspectives. They operate with integrity and make decisions based on fairness and the greater good rather than personal gain.

But they aren't so focused on the heart that they lose focus on the work. They have to keep a clear vision for the organization's success and long-term sustainability. When their people reach full potential, the company does too.

As we get closer to the end of our careers, it's not uncommon for leaders to feel out of touch with the world a little bit. As fast as technology is changing, it's hard to keep up with everything and lead at the same time. Sometimes people are tempted to try and fake their way through it until retirement and hope nobody notices. But here's the thing. You can't leave a legacy as someone you aren't. No matter how hard we try to be someone we think we want to be, our true selves are always at the root of our legacy. Authenticity and vulnerability are key. I can't tell you how many times I have said, "It is a strength of leaders to ask for help, not a weakness."

This is how people come to trust you. You have to be straight with them. If you don't know something, it's best to admit that you don't know it, ask someone to help you with it, and learn it. This demonstrates that you are self-aware and willing to learn, thereby setting (and keeping) a standard of excellence. After all, aren't these the qualities you want your people to have?

When you do this, they are more willing to come to you when they recognize their own weaknesses. One of the greatest servant leaders I know is my close friend Eric Thornburg. He had some very wise observations about what this means:

> In our society, there are certain expectations that come with being in a C-Suite position. But the responsibilities should serve as the foundation for our behaviors and actions. This informs how we lead and follow the servant leadership model. You may be at the top of the organization chart, but it really needs to be flipped upside down so that the people who are traditionally at the bottom are at the top. This way, you're serving and supporting them.
>
> My faith also informs the way I serve. It has given me a lot of fortitude and stamina to know that I can survive the difficult times. As Christians, both Nick and I just trust and lean into this. Faith has been an enormous part of our stories, and I think when we're leading in our workplaces, you can see the evidence of that. But neither of us wear it on our sleeves, if you know what I mean.
>
> If you are a new CEO and expect everybody to carry you around on their shoulders, you're in for a rude awakening. Our responsibilities definitely humble us along the way. It

is important that every single person who works for you knows that while you might not be pleased with an outcome, or you may not be happy with someone's performance, at the end of the day, it's really about trusting relationships you have built with them.

There's a lot of consequences to leadership. You have people's lives, their careers, and their families' welfare at stake. I think both Nick and I witnessed a lot of things that just didn't feel right or look right when we were first coming into our careers. A lot of people didn't really know where they stood and were fearful. This was in the early eighties, so things were a little different. I think we both thought, "Gosh, if we were ever fortunate enough to be in senior leadership roles, we have to make sure people authentically trust us and know where they stand. In some cases that means that they can make change and get better or chose not to continue to invest in the company and move on to the next one."

We learned to embrace real, straight talk with people so we could build trust with them. This meant sharing hard truths sometimes. I don't like doing it, but I always feel good when I've sat down with somebody and said, "OK, I want to talk to you. Here's how X is affecting the organization and your reputation. Let's talk about how we can work on that."

It's hard, but that's building trust. Not just with that person, but then the rest of the team in the organization sees we are dealing with these difficult situations in the business.

Many great leaders have taken the traditional organizational chart and flipped it upside down. If the CEO was at the top and the workers were at the bottom, they now place the workers at the top and the CEO at the bottom. This reminds them that they are stewards of those above them and that everything they do should be to benefit those who carry the company on their shoulders.

There is a great deal of research out there on vulnerability and authenticity for leaders. Bookshelves are stuffed with publications that teach us how to harness these qualities and why they are important. I don't need to recreate them here, but I do want to share my observation that when leaders are willing to show their true selves, including their fears, weaknesses, and struggles, it creates an environment where everyone feels safe. It creates a sense of relatability and makes leaders more approachable. This, in turn, strengthens their connection with team members and allows the team to better understand that it's OK to make mistakes. So, decisions can come from a place of courage rather than fear.

Vulnerability allows leaders to understand the struggles and challenges of others. When this happens, they can better respond to individual needs and provide the most appropriate support. Leaders who openly admit their mistakes and seek feedback create a space where new, creative ideas and perspectives can flourish. This also allows leaders to embrace uncertainty and change. It shows that it's OK to not know. This helps everyone come together in adapting to new circumstances with greater flexibility and resilience.

It's important to note that this doesn't mean sharing every personal detail or being emotionally exposed all the time. You have to find a balance to know when to show vulnerability and when to be confident in your leadership skills. This is not an easy balance to find sometimes, but with practice, I know you'll be able to find it. And when you do, those who look up to you will find it as well.

Reflection Points

- Have you ever had a time when you were fired or another employee you were close with was fired? How did it feel?

- As a leader, what do you want to do to make your company better, and what are some of the specific steps you need to take to get there?

- How can your team members help you to accomplish this? Are you doing everything you can to help them realize their full potential?

CHAPTER 9

Who's Saying Your Name?

As you near retirement, you are less and less involved in the day-to-day operations of your organization. You know fewer people by name when you walk into the office, and you notice that you are losing touch with some of the finer details that you used to know. If you're completely honest with yourself, you would admit that there are parts of the company that are fairly mysterious to you at this point.

But perhaps that's a good thing. After all, you have built a team you can trust 100 percent to handle their jobs well. And if there is a problem, you hope they know they can bring it to you, and you'll help them in every way you can. You continue to focus on the 10,000-foot view and leave the details to everyone else.

But then one day, you are sitting in a meeting and realize that nobody has actually said your name. Not once. Nobody asks you a question. Nobody defers to your judgment. Nobody looks to you for advice. You might as well not even be there.

For the rest of the week, you take careful note of how often you hear anyone speak your name. The answer is hardly ever. Do your employees even know who you are? Why are you even coming to work anymore?

As you get closer to retirement, you start to wonder, will they miss you? What kind of gap will you leave? Will it be big? Will it be barely noticeable? Will it be hard to fill?

Then your mind starts to turn to darker thoughts. Do they even like you? Do they want you gone? Are they just waiting until you finally decide to retire before they bring in someone they actually want to work with?

You are faced with that same question that has been with you since the beginning of your career—what kind of value are you bringing every day?

Your colleagues are all talking about leaving a legacy and maintaining their reputation as they plan for their exit. You wonder what kind of legacy you are going to leave. You're at the end of the career, so you can't change your brand now! It's been set. Now is the time to reap the effects of what you put in all these years.

Who is going to be saying your name after you go?

Mentorship

One of the best ways to leave a lasting impact on those who come behind you is to be a mentor. Before you retire, you can be on the constant lookout for ways to speak on behalf of others in rooms where they are not invited yet, to promote promising young people with other leaders.

Some people think of mentorship as this official agreement between two people, one at the middle or end of their career and the other just starting out. While that may be the case in some instances, mentorship doesn't have to be so strictly defined.

Mentorship is one of the core aspects of servant leadership—to give more than you take every day of your life. The cool thing is that when you give 100 percent, you will receive 200 percent back. It's like the most magical formula ever, and it works in all relationships. Your spouse, your kids, your friends all have dynamics of mentorship in them. Sometimes you are the mentor, and sometimes you are the mentee. Remember my high school principal? The one I mentioned in the first chapter? He was the first mentor I had outside my own family. His influence still resonates with me, even now decades later. We can't underestimate the power of good mentors.

At work, I promise you will get better results with your coworkers when you focus on their personal growth and development more than your own. This is, in a way, mentorship. Good things just happen when you do the right thing without looking for a return.

Mentorship can happen in the briefest moments. I have found myself feeling prompted to say a kind word to a stranger sometimes. Why? For the simple fact that I could tell they needed a little encouragement. It cost me nothing, but it might make their day. We all have those opportunities every day. And you might be surprised how many times people say to me, "Hey, I know you!"

I honestly don't remember them, but then they say, "Well, you were in here last year and you said something nice to me, and I never forgot it."

You never know how many missed opportunities we all have every day that make the world a little bit better by encouraging people without expecting anything in return. My friend Valoria Armstrong found this out when she left her last company:

> You never really know the impact you have on others. When
> I made the announcement that I was leaving my company, I

was amazed how many people reached out and thanked me. One woman reached out to me who I had talked to years ago. She sent me a message that said, "Valoria, I just want to thank you." I remembered a conversation we had about a very personal decision she was making. She said that conversation had really impacted her in so many ways, and she just wanted to thank me for taking time to talk with her. Sometimes it's the smallest things that make the biggest impact, and we don't even know it.

In some instances, a long-term relationship is the best opportunity for mentorship. Friendships can be the most powerful mentorship opportunities in our lives when you surround yourself with people who love you and fill your goodwill jar. I asked a few of my dearest friends to share their thoughts about mentorship, and I am excited to pass them along to you.

My friend Susan Lancho reflected on what mentorship meant in her life:

I've been very fortunate over the years with terrific mentors. My first boss was a seasoned professional within ten years of retirement. I was young, right out of college, and he pushed me to take on new challenges. For example, one day he said, I'd like for you to be the MC of our all-employee meetings from now on—that was something he had been doing. We're talking an office of probably 250 people, and I'm thinking, "Are you kidding me?"

He did this and other things like it because he saw something in me that I didn't see in myself, and I needed a push. I remind myself now that I'm in a leadership position and that's the kind of leader I want to be. I want to be able to help someone else discover their strengths and gain confidence. I want to be the one to say, "You can do it. I believe in you."

As a leader, you help others secure the tools and skills they need, help them learn from their mistakes, and you let them grow. There can be a real satisfaction in seeing someone develop.

I have been closely involved in the career of my friend, Attorney-at-Law, LaToi Mayo. I asked her what she thought of our relationship, and this is what she said:

From the first time I met Nick twenty years ago, he has mentored me about balancing my professionalism in law while still maintaining who I am. He's also opened doors for me in opportunities to advance my career. Mentoring includes talks over lunches and dinners and sharing time and conversations about personal and professional goals and endeavors. Nick helps me take my goals one step further and gives me the opportunity to make those goals come to fruition anywhere he can.

When I was a young lawyer, kind of fresh out of school, I didn't really know the proper protocol on how to approach business leaders and maintain professionalism without seeming awkward. I routinely bounced things off Nick. He has not only been a professional mentor; he's also been a personal mentor and friend of mine.

He taught me to keep faith, maintain a professional tone, and still get the work done irrespective of particular personal opinion.

You have to be like that or be that way to be a true leader. You must always feel like your audience believes that they're being heard and valued. At the end of the day, I know for sure and for certain Nick's going to do what's right versus what's best for the bottom dollar. That's what being a leader is all about.

He's taught me that, just as he does for me, I need to do for others with respect to young lawyers and young individuals seeking to find their place and make a career. I do a lot in this regard with our mentor/mentee program in my organization now. Even if I can't do a lot, I do take any opportunity to sit down and talk with younger people. I try to see if I can help because I know how important it is, especially among African American females where I live. I see them trying to break into industries where they quite frankly don't see a lot of themselves among the ranks. So it's my turn to pay it forward.

Her words here have brought me so much joy. The ripple in the pond is continuing!

Leaving a Legacy

We're building our legacies every single day. No matter what age you are—if you're young, a teenager, or you're a retired person with more days behind you than in front of you—it doesn't really matter. It doesn't matter where you come from; it's all about where you finish. We each build our legacies every day that we are alive by how we impact our families, our friends, our neighbors, our company, and our coworkers. I started building my legacy, like most people do, in elementary school. Then through high school, through college, through my work history, and in all the places we lived during my career. I didn't know it, but I was building a legacy the whole time.

You know I came from humble beginnings. That doesn't matter at all. To this day, I love to go back to my hometown in Kentucky, and although my parents are deceased, people still come up to me to say, "Hey, Nick! Your family was always hardworking. Your parents treated everyone right. They were good people."

That kind of reputation comes from a history of doing things right and treating people well. Notice it has nothing to do with financial wherewithal or job history. It's about making those good choices every day for your whole life. You can't reach a certain point and say, "OK, now I'm retired. I've treated people terrible. I've moved all around the country and never built any relationships, but now I'm going to start treating people right."

No. Your legacy has already been built. History doesn't disappear. The good and bad and ugly behind you don't go away. Think about what you're doing right now. Are you trying to make people around you better? Are you genuinely wanting to lift those around you up before yourself?

The scenario in the story at the start of this chapter is what many CEOs and other leaders go through when they face closing out their career. Have they actually accomplished every single thing they had hoped to do as a leader? Probably not. Life doesn't work that way. But we can all work to leave a positive impact. Think of the way a stone dropped in a calm pond starts a ripple that moves out to the shore—we can make a difference that impacts the lives of others well beyond our immediate sphere of influence.

Leaving a legacy starts way back before our first job. It is in our values, our foundation, and how we treat people. It's the tough things we have to do. It's strengthened by the character we have as we live our values and add value to every relationship. With every drop in the goodwill jar, we are building the legacy that will remain when we leave. As we do this, we can feel at peace, knowing we have contributed to something greater than ourselves. A legacy can inspire future generations to carry forward the values and ideals you have worked your whole life to share. Everything that we put out comes back to us.

At the end of the day, if nobody ever says your name, does it even matter what else you've done? Because you really haven't influenced people's lives if they can't remember you. Will they say you were a great neighbor? Will they say you were kind? Will they say you were a giver, not a taker?

In my opinion, that's really the measuring stick of success. Maybe someone is going to have more money than I'll ever have. They might have a nicer car, bigger house—all that. But you know, if they haven't left anything in the goodwill jar of anyone else, it doesn't really matter. Remember back in chapter 2 when I talked about the mansion standing next to the most rundown shack you have ever seen? Both houses had the same grave out front. That's the whole point. We're all going to the same place.

It is not just the difference that we are making at work. It's the difference we're making in our neighborhoods, our churches, our kids' soccer teams. Everywhere we go. If you're in your neighborhood association, are you making your community a little bit better? Does anyone know your name? Are you making a positive difference?

Think of what happens when you move away. What are people saying about you after you go? Are they saying, "I'm so glad those people moved. They never had anything to do with us. What was their name again?" Or are they sad you left and wishing to see you again, saying your name with praise and honor?

Have you ever watched as a disgruntled employee threatens others with their retirement? "I'm going to leave this company. Then you'll all see."

I kind of laugh at this. See what? That we'll be happier without you? Yup. We'll see alright. They don't realize that we're secretly watching the calendar, waiting for the day they leave so we can celebrate.

Or a disgruntled neighbor says, "I can't wait to move out of this neighborhood and get away from these people."

Or at the church they say, "I'm going to leave this church and these people. Just you wait and see."

Well, the truth is, "these people" can't wait for them to leave. We all want to be around good, fun-loving people who offer kindness. If you're one of these grumps, we can't wait for you to go. Our church been around 130 years; it's probably going to be all right without you.

My family has lived in many communities, such as Kentucky, West Virginia, Virginia, Pennsylvania, and Missouri, and we can honestly say they were all good. Why were they all good? Because we made the best out of it. We tried to add value everywhere we lived, so we didn't really have any bad experiences because we never let it into our lives. We focused on enjoying each place we lived, and we hoped that we always left people with saying, "We hope the Rowes move back some day."

If nobody is saying your name after you go, what kind of life have you lived? You can have all the money in the world and still have absolutely nothing. At the end of the day, if nobody knows who you are, it won't matter what title you held or what your salary was. Remember the shoeshine guy? He's leaving a legacy with everyone he meets because he loves them. It's that easy.

When he retires (if he retires!), nobody is going to be talking about his house or his car or his saving account. For all I know, he's a millionaire with a private jet! None of that matters. I just remember how he treated me every time he saw me. He filled my goodwill jar, and even though our relationship was brief, it stayed with me.

If you are a leader now, you're clearly good about taking care of yourself and promoting yourself enough to get where you are. But have you ever asked yourself if you're good about anybody else? It's one thing to know your superiors, but do you know people who serve you all the time? Do you know the custodian's name? Do you know the name of the security guard? They work there, just like everybody else. They're doing the exact same thing that you're doing. They're feeding families and paying bills. I always say, "Leave your title at the door, and everything else will work out."

This doesn't just pertain to executives. It's for everyone. I knew someone who was CEO for years in an organization. I learned that his spouse never connected with anyone at her husband's company at all. She would come to the office to visit him and walk right past everyone at the office without ever greeting them. She'd say to his receptionist, "I'm here to see John," and stand there as cold as a stranger. For years!

To think about a CEO whose spouse never even acknowledged the people around seems too sad. That receptionist confessed that it really hurt her feelings. It was like she didn't matter at all. How easy would it have been for that spouse to say, "Hey, how's your day going? How's your family? Did you have a good weekend?"

Can you imagine the goodwill that would have built not only between the two of them but for that CEO as well? We all have those opportunities. Good things happen when you surround yourself with very good people. And one way to do that is to bring out the good in them.

I have mentioned my good friend Eric Thornburg a few times in this book. His father was a highly successful utility executive, and when I was a very young manager, I was invited to attend a big conference where he spoke. The only thing I knew about him at the time was that he was a tall guy with a handlebar mustache.

The event was held at a rodeo ranch where a huge crowd was invited to come and have dinner. He spoke to the crowd and announced his retirement while we were eating. At the end, someone got up and said, "We have arranged a few buses to take you all back to your hotel. They are waiting out front, if you want to leave. If you'd like to say something to Mr. Thornburg, you're welcome to stay after for a little bit."

Nobody got on the bus. Everybody got in line to shake Mr. Thornburg's hand. I knew most of the people there hadn't ever worked for that guy, so why'd everybody get in line? It touched me to see how many lives he had touched beyond his own company. As I learned more about him, I found out it was the way he had led that touched everyone. He had a Christian spirit in the way he taught people.

That was a defining moment for me. I never will forget it. Even though it was forty years ago, it gave me an idea of the kind of leader I wanted to be one day.

Vision of Retirement

Too many CEOs and presidents and executives think that the company will absolutely crumble when they leave, but guess what? The organization is going to go on without you. They are going to be just fine. When I retired after forty years, I was sent a lot of emails and text messages. Not a single one was about my title or even the job I did. Nobody remembers that. Instead, they were nice notes, saying things like, "Twenty years ago, you said something to me when my husband had cancer, and it meant the world to me." I don't remember what I said, but it made a difference.

People remember the way you treated them. Remember, we are all making impact on each other's lives every single day. It's the little things that help in the very moment they need them that matter most.

I've been to funerals for people who gave their whole lives to work, and guess what? The churches were empty, because they never bothered to create lasting relationships. They never filled anyone's goodwill jar. It's always a humbling reminder to me of what we leave behind. What do people say about you when you're not around?

More than ever, our world today needs more givers. It needs more hope. It needs more compassion. And it needs more kindness. We're all human. We need to treat each other as such. Are you sharing kindness? Are you giving hope? Are you inspiring people? Whose life have you improved?

Imagine! If we had more people who ask themselves these questions, the world will be a pretty good place to live.

At the end of the day, if nobody ever says your name, it doesn't matter what else you've done. As you strive to fill the goodwill jar, you will affect more people than you'll ever know. This book is my way of trying to fill your goodwill jar. I hope you close it and go out today to look for ways to fill up that goodwill jar of the next person you see. And the next. And the next.

There is no end to the good each of us can do every single day.

Points to Live By

- To make this world a better place, the majority of us have to continue to do the right thing.

- Live a life of inspiration.

- Leave something good behind wherever you go.

- Touch someone every day.

- Listen more. Talk less.

- Draw from the positive places, not the negative.

- The higher you go in a company or organization, the more you need the Lord's guidance.

- In the end it will be OK; if it is not OK, it is not the end.

- Do what you say you are going to do. Your word is everything.

- Live your values even more as a leader.

- Create contagious happiness everywhere you go.

- Keep filling the goodwill jar!

REFLECTIONS

ON YOUR LIFE

So, here you are. You might look at yourself in the mirror and realize you are who you are. There's no going back now.

You sit out on the patio, the back porch, maybe by the pool or at the beach and you wonder, "Who is saying my name?" And "Did I make a difference in people's lives?"

Your career is coming to an end, and you ask yourself how you led? What will your legacy be? Did you lead with inspiration? Believe me, this time comes sooner than you think.

Remember, your brand has been established over the years. How many relationships did you build? Did you add value as an employee, as a friend, as a coworker, in your community and neighborhood, to your company/organization, in your family, and in your marriage or long-term relationships?

You were rooted in a solid foundation. What did you do with those opportunities? Did you build trust with people along life's journey? Were you a giver versus a taker?

All these thoughts run through your mind as you play the back nine holes of life's golf course. You begin to wonder, "Am I on Hole #10? #14? Or am I on the last Hole—#18?"

Only God knows.

After having read this book, I'm hopeful that we all reflect on how we lived our lives.

I cannot judge anyone, but I try to take this imperfect human being of myself and make my earthly time worthy of a decent legacy.

I'm hopeful that *The Goodwill Jar* has inspired and tugged at your heart. Now, let's keep filling it until the Grace and Mercy that our Savior has given us have ended, and He takes us to the Goodwill Home in Heaven that awaits.

Thank you for sharing this journey with me. Now, I hope you go out and continue to live the best life you possibly can, filling the jar of everyone you meet.

ACKNOWLEDGMENTS

Thanks to all the good people and family members who have contributed to my success. First is my family, with my wife, Tyra, and daughters, Dominique and Ebony. I am also very thankful for Jackie Joyner-Kersee for the time she took when she inspired me with her discussion around "winning."

I also want to thank Eric Thornburg, Ashli Watts, Bruce Hauk, Valoria Armstrong, Sam Henry, Brian Queen, Susan Lancho, Traci Cross, LaToi Mayo, and Stacy Owens. Without their willingness to contribute, this book would have lacked the depth and richness I had hoped to add.

Special thanks to my writing partner, Heidi Scott, for her tireless efforts to help me produce this book.

Lastly, thank you to the Advantage team for walking alongside me through this whole process. The world needs us right now to put more in that Goodwill Jar!

ABOUT THE AUTHOR

Nick O. Rowe was the president of Kentucky American Water, the largest investor-owned water utility in the state, providing high-quality and reliable water and/or wastewater services to approximately half a million people. In this role, he reinforced and strengthened customer, regulatory, and local government relationships, drove operational and financial results, and was the principal external contact for American Water in Kentucky. He was responsible for driving performance within the state, establishing consistent best practices and enhancing American Water's efforts to maintain and build external relationships. Additionally, Rowe served as the senior vice president of American Water, overseeing the operations of Tennessee, Virginia, and Maryland American Water.

Rowe joined American Water in 1987 as a management assistant at West Virginia American Water and was subsequently promoted to various management positions with responsibility for the day-to-day operations of American Water facilities in Pennsylvania and oversight of contract operations in North Carolina, Georgia, and Florida. Similar to his current role, Rowe previously served as the senior vice president of American Water's Central and Eastern divisions, which included the states of Illinois, Indiana, Iowa, Maryland, Michigan, Missouri, New York, Ohio, Virginia, and West Virginia. He also served as the chief diversity officer and vice president of Business Change for American Water.

Rowe was involved with various regulatory agencies, civic organizations, and professional associations and currently holds board positions with Lexington Industrial Foundation, Central Bank Advisory Board, Kentucky Chamber of Commerce (past chair), and Lexington Clinic. He previously served on the boards of Commerce Lexington (past chair), United Way of the Bluegrass, and St. Louis Regional Chamber of Commerce. He was a member of American Water Works Association (AWWA), the National Association of Water Companies, and the national AWWA Water Utility Council.

Rowe holds a bachelor's degree in engineering from Western Kentucky University and a master's degree in business administration from Lebanon Valley College. He attended executive education programs at Oxford University in England and the International Institute for Management Development (IMD) in Lausanne, Switzerland.

In July 2007, the Public Relations Society of America's Thoroughbred Chapter selected Rowe to receive its Communicator of the Year Award. He was selected for his leadership and open communication in the business.